RAISING A
THINKING CHILD
WORKBOOK

RAISING A
THINKING CHILD
WORKBOOK

MYRNA B. SHURE, PH.D.

with Theresa Foy Digeronimo, M.Ed.

• • •

Illustrations by Jackie Aher

An Owl Book

Henry Holt and Company
New York

Henry Holt and Company, Inc.
Publishers since 1866
115 West 18th Street
New York, New York 10011

Henry Holt® is a registered
trademark of Henry Holt and Company, Inc.

Published in Canada by Fitzhenry & Whiteside Ltd.,
195 Allstate Parkway, Markham, Ontario L3R 4T8.

Library of Congress Cataloging-in-Publication Data
Shure, Myrna B.
Raising a thinking child : help your young child to resolve
everyday conflicts and get along with others / Myrna B. Shure with
Theresa Foy DiGeronimo—1st ed.
      p.   cm.
Includes index.
1. Interpersonal conflict in children.   2. Problem solving in
children.   3. Social skills in children.   4. Childrearing.
I. DiGeronimo, Theresa Foy.   II. Title.
BF723.I645S487   1994   94-5166
649'.1—dc20   CIP

ISBN 0-8050-4383-7

Henry Holt books are available for special promotions
and premiums. For details contact: Director, Special Markets.

First Owl Book edition—1996

Designed by Betty Lew

Printed in the United States of America
All first editions are printed on acid-free paper. ∞

1 3 5 7 9 10 8 6 4 2

❧ Contents ❧

PART 2: CHILD/CHILD SITUATIONS   107

❧ Acknowledgments ❧

The problem-solving approach developed for *Raising a Thinking Child Workbook* is based on twenty-five years of research with children at home and in schools, made possible by grants from the Applied Research Branch and the Prevention Research Branch of the National Institute of Mental Health, Washington, D.C.

Very special recognition goes to George Spivack, whose original research established an important link between interpersonal problem-solving skills and behavior in adolescents—research that led to our joint efforts to discover this link in younger children—and inspired me to create the activities and games developed in this workbook.

It was the help and creative contributions of many people that made possible the research, service delivery, and evaluations of what became the I Can Problem Solve (ICPS) interventions. The former administrators of the Philadelphia Get Set Day Care program—Dr. Jeffrey O. Jones, Director; Rosemary Mazzatenta, Assistant Director; Dr. Lafayette Powell, Chief, Psychological Services; and Vivian Ray, Chief Psychologist—paved the way in 1968 for our very first research projects with both teachers and parents of preschoolers.

Deep appreciation is expressed to Dr. Constance Clayton, former Superintendent; Leontine D. Scott, former Associate Superintendent of School Operations; and Dr. Irvin J. Farber, former Director of Research, School District of Philadelphia, for their help with and support of our research in the schools throughout the years.

I am also indebted to principals of elementary schools throughout the city of Philadelphia who supported our recent research with parents of six- and seven-year-olds, and to the parent coordinators for their efforts in recruiting parents to participate: Blankenburg Elementary School, Dr. Agnes Barksdale, principal, and Vivian Chestang, parent coordinator; W. D. Kelley Elementary School, Anthony Bellos, principal, and Chantala Clark, parent coordinator; Locke Elementary School, Janet Samuels, principal, and Frances Carter, parent coordinator; Martha Washington Elementary School, Dr. Harold Trawick, principal, and Jesse Carter, parent coordinator.

Much insight about helping parents learn ICPS was given to me by Virginia Jamison, an Instructional Support Teacher who, in addition to training teachers in the Philadelphia public schools, also taught ICPS to all the parent trainers in the more than two hundred schools in the School District of Philadelphia. I am also indebted to Dr. Kathryn Healey, now at the Institute for Graduate Clinical Psychology at Widener University, and Phyllis Ditlow, education coordinator for the Philadelphia Prekindergarten Head Start program, who help me train teachers and parents around the country and who continually come up with new ideas for ICPS games and exercises.

Gerry Langgut, Laura Caravello, and Dr. Eileen Altman, prevention coordinators at the Mental Health Association in Illinois (MHAI), implemented ICPS for many years with teachers and have added important insights for its use with parents as well. I thank Jan Holcomb, Executive Director, MHAI; Ann Nerad, Project Founder and former MHAI board president and member; Dr. Edith Fifer, Administrator for Early Childhood Special Education Programs, Chicago Public Schools; and Dr. James G. Kelly, professor of psychology at the University of Illinois at Chicago and Project Consultant for MHAI. Appreciation also goes to two Chicago public schools for their pioneering ICPS parent training there: Schubert Elementary School, Cynthia Wnek, principal; and Hartigan Elementary School, Betty Greer, principal. I would like to give special recognition to Diane Kacprzak, a Chicago parent who provided leadership to and sparked enthusiasm in other parents in that city, and to Sandra Hinely, a community resource consultant at the DuPage County Illinois Health Department who originally planted the seed to create more hands-on activities for parents and children such as those that appear in this workbook. It was Bonnie Aberson, a school psychologist in Dade County, Florida, who in her years of experience implementing ICPS with parents and teachers has successfully adapted the program for use with special-needs youngsters, including those with Attention Deficit Hyperactivity Disorder (ADHD). Appreciation also goes to Onetha J. Gilliard, director of Region VI Operations, Dade County Public Schools, for her support of parent training in that locale.

A particularly special tribute goes to Phyllis Ditlow, who, as mentioned earlier, not only helps me train parents and teachers but played an important role in helping me create some of the activities for this workbook. Her unique talents made possible the exercises that make the problem-solving approach easy to absorb for parents, and activities that children can both learn from and have fun with at the same time.

I thank Theresa DiGeronimo for helping to make this workbook easy to use; Jackie Aher for her drawings that helped bring the exercises to life; and Betty Lew for her design of this book. I also thank Lynn Seligman, my agent, for her enthusiastic support in making this project a reality. Cynthia Vartan, my editor at Henry Holt, worked overtime and must have been on automatic pilot to see the myriad details that needed attention before this workbook could reach its final form. And to Carrie Smith, whose fine-tooth comb gave it its finishing touches, I am very grateful.

But it was the bold and fearless accounts by our ICPS parents with the problem-solving approach that contributed so much, and it is to them and their children that I dedicate this newest creation, *Raising a Thinking Child Workbook*.

RAISING A
THINKING CHILD
WORKBOOK

Introduction

✤

What do you do when your child

- won't listen to you, or do what you ask?
- hits other children, or takes away their toys?

Why do some children do well in school, and others don't?

In more than twenty-five years of working with families with young children, my research colleague George Spivack and I learned that in families of all income levels, children as young as age three or four can learn to solve everyday problems that arise with others. We also learned that children who are able to think for themselves are better adjusted than those who cannot or do not, and that good problem solvers are less likely to show aggression or withdraw socially and are more likely to develop empathy and care about others, be good leaders, and have friends.

Why is it important for young children to be good problem solvers? Because research now reveals that children who show impulsive and withdrawn behaviors, and who are having difficulty making friends, are at risk for later, more serious problems that we are all concerned about today: violence, drug use, teen pregnancy, school dropout, and some forms of psychological dysfunction, including depression.

Although telling children what to do, and even explaining why, may result in their doing what you want, often this compliance does not last. Perhaps that's because they've heard the explanations many times before and are now tuning out. Perhaps it's because we are doing the thinking for them. We all want to be free to think for ourselves. And, I have learned, so do very young children—if they have the skills and the freedom to do it.

My approach does not teach children what to do and why, but rather, it teaches them *how* to think so they can decide for themselves what and what not to do, and why. How parents can help their children learn *how* to think, not what to think, and how this improves behavior problems, or prevents them from occurring at all, is described in my book *Raising a Thinking Child: Help Your Young Child to Resolve Everyday Conflicts and Get Along with Others* (Henry Holt and Company, 1994; paperback, Pocket Books, 1996). In that book I outlined how even very young children can learn to solve everyday problems that come up with other people by practicing a series of thinking skills from a program I call I Can Problem Solve, or ICPS. *Raising a Thinking Child Workbook* is an outgrowth of that book.

WHO IS THIS WORKBOOK FOR?

This workbook is for parents and children to use together. Please be aware that the word *parent* means any adult—mom, dad, grandparent, or guardian—who wants to teach their children how to think about solving their problems. Most of the activities and games are for children aged four to seven, but children slightly younger or slightly older will enjoy them too. Some of the early games can include children even as young as two, or who have just begun to speak.

Children in many schools across the country receive training in the I Can Problem Solve curricula designed for the classroom. This workbook can help the parents of these children reinforce the classroom lessons at home. Parent educators can also use this workbook in systematic training meetings held in schools or mental health settings, and clinicians have found that the techniques in the I Can Problem Solve program offer a new approach to family therapy as well.

WHAT DOES THIS WORKBOOK DO?

- It reinforces your children's efforts to think for themselves.
- It gives you practical ways to teach your children social and emotional competencies.
- It gives you and your children many hands-on things to do that help them become (a) more *empathetic*, (b) better able to *cope with frustration and disappointment*, and (c) better *problem solvers*.
- It gives you a place to record how your children are progressing in problem-solving skills and behavior.
- It gives you many ways to practice problem-solving talk with your children.
- It helps you keep track of your own progress as an ICPS parent.

HOW TO USE THIS WORKBOOK

Because the I Can Problem Solve approach builds skills step by step, you should start at the beginning and work your way to the end. Do only those games your children can understand and enjoy. You may skip those that are too difficult, but it is important not to skip whole sections. A four-year-old, for example, might not understand the word *frustrated*, which is used in some of the games to help children think about feelings, but probably will understand words such as *happy*, *sad*, or *mad*. You can judge how far your children can be challenged, without pushing too hard. When you finish the program, you can then go back and keep repeating in any order the games your children especially liked. Even months later you can try games previously skipped that your children might now understand, or repeat successfully completed activities for more depth of understanding.

Throughout the workbook there are a number of suggested parent scripts. Use a flexible approach to these scripts. You do not need to read them word for word. If you like, you can create your own games and activities, but you should do this only after you thoroughly understand what your children are learning, and why.

The only materials you will need are crayons and pencils. In some of the activities the crayons have a specific purpose, but in others they are simply to be used to color the pictures if your children want to.

If you're using the workbook with more than one child, just duplicate those pages on which you record your children's responses. You may also wish to duplicate pages that the children want to color so that all children have their own copy.

Parts of the Workbook

You'll see that the workbook is divided into two parts, parent/child problems and child/child problems.

Typical parent/child problems include:

- child won't clean her room
- child jumps on the furniture
- child interrupts you while you're on the phone

Parent/child problems are normal in all families. This section gives you and your children practice at solving these common kinds of problems, and also less common ones that may be unique in your home.

Typical child/child problems include:

- two children fight over a toy
- one child feels left out of a play group
- one child teases or intimidates another child

This section lets children practice ICPS thinking skills in settling their own disputes.

Each of the above sections is divided into two parts: activities for your children, and activities for you alone, called Parent's Pages that will help you practice the "ICPS dialoguing" way of talking with your children. Both of these parts are important. One helps your children become skilled at solving problems, the other helps you become skilled at helping them do that. As you move through the workbook you will find it easy to learn how to talk with your children the problem-solving way if you become actively involved with the Parent Pages in *each* section before going on to the next set of activities with your child.

In the back of the workbook you'll find word-pair posters containing some of the ICPS words that you'll be "playing" with. You can tear them out or duplicate them and hang them on the walls in your children's rooms or on the refrigerator. They will serve as reminders of the special ICPS words we use that will later help children solve problems. You may wish to make your own posters for the remaining ICPS words.

TIME AND TIMING

Children will get the most out of the activities in the workbook when they are having fun. Start by spending only five or ten minutes with an exercise and try to build up to twenty or thirty minutes each day, depending on your children's levels of interest. Stop when your children become restless.

Go through the workbook at a pace that is comfortable for your children. If the early games are too easy, go through them more quickly, but don't skip them entirely; they're needed for association with later games.

If possible, set up a regular time each day for the activities and games in the workbook; regularity helps to establish a comfortable routine. You may soon find that after several days of announcing "It's ICPS time," whether that time is after school or before bed, your children may well remind you of it if you forget. Once your children learn the lessons, the words and ideas from those lessons can be used anywhere: in the car, at the grocery store, and at home.

BECOMING AN ICPS FAMILY

In my book *Raising a Thinking Child*, I describe an ICPS family whose two children, ages four and six, go through the program step by step and how their two year old sibling joins in on the early games. I show how the impulsive and sometimes aggressive son walks through the steps that transform his thinking processes and make him an "ICPSer" and how his sister, a naturally good problem solver, gets even better at it. I also show how a six-year-old friend, who is shy and sometimes fearful of others, joins in.

The goal of this workbook is to give you lots of ideas and opportunities to practice the I Can Problem Solve program so you can become an ICPS family too. Your older children can help teach the younger ones so that everyone in the house participates. The workbook will help you guide your children to identify problems, care more about their own and others' feelings, realize that what they do has an impact on other people, and, most important, that there is more than one way to solve a problem. While you will become more sensitive to what's on your children's minds and how they are feeling, your children will become more sensitive to what is on your mind and how you are feeling too.

When you finish the workbook you'll find a certificate that declares you an official ICPS family. This is not a trite or meaningless title. ICPS families are different from other families in many ways. In ICPS families

- children learn *how* to think, not what to think.
- children learn to think through a problem, so they can decide on a solution in light of its impact on themselves and others.
- children are empowered with skills that enable them to negotiate more successfully for what they want, and to cope with the frustration when they can't have what they want.
- parents are empowered with skills that enable them to help their children become effective problem solvers.
- children grow up to be thinking and feeling human beings who behave not out of fear of punishment but out of a genuine desire to not want to hurt themselves or others.

Happy ICPSing!

• Part 1 •

Parent/Child Situations

❧

I'm sure that every single day you find yourself, like all parents, in some conflict situation with your children. Maybe they want attention while you're cooking dinner, or maybe they won't go to bed on time. These are typical situations that can be handled in lots of different ways. You can demand, command, or ignore those behaviors in the hope that they will go away. You can suggest, model, or even explain to your children what they should or should not do, and why. Or, you can use the I Can Problem Solve approach.

In Part 1 of this workbook, you'll find lots of ICPS games and activities that will help you and your children think about your conflicts and solve them without resorting to anger, hostility, or withdrawal.

You'll see that the parent/child situations are divided into the rooms of your house. The games begin in the kitchen, move to the bedroom, then on to the bathroom, and finish up in the living room/family room. It's important to do the games in the order presented because each room, illustrated by problems specific to that room, emphasizes a different part of the ICPS approach that builds upon the one before it. Except for the games where children point to and color pictures of objects, the games will be more fun if you play them in the actual room for which they are designed.

In the first room, the workbook emphasizes carefully chosen words, called ICPS Words, that will set the stage for later problem solving; in the second room, the ICPS Words help children to recognize and react to another's feelings; in the third room, ICPS Words and feelings are combined to consider solutions to behaviors; and finally, in the fourth room, ICPS Words, feelings, and solutions are all used to think about the consequences to actions.

You will find Parent's Pages at the end of each section. These activities will help you polish your skills as an ICPS parent. As with the children's activities, the emphasis in each section highlights one skill that builds upon the one before.

Beginning Parent Log

❧

Before beginning the exercises and activities in this first section, fill out Log A$_1$. This same log appears again as A$_2$ at the end of Part 1, so you can see your and your children's progress as you move through the pages of this workbook. The first line of the log is filled out as an example.

1. *Problem Situation:* Jot down something your child recently did that caused a conflict, such as jumping on furniture, eating candy before dinner, or any problem unique to you and your own family.

2. *Parent Actions/Statements/Questions:* Write a quick note about what you did or said when the problem arose.

3. *Child's Responses:* Note what your child did or said.

4. *Conclusion:* Did your child comply or resist? If resist, what did you do or say?

5. *Outcome:* Write a positive sign for a positive outcome, a zero for a neutral outcome, and a negative sign for a negative outcome. You may wish to add a note saying how you felt about the way you handled the situation and how you think your child felt.

LOG A₁

I Can Problem Solve (ICPS): Parent and Child Exchanges

Date	Problem Situation	Parent Actions/ Statements/Questions	Child's Responses	Conclusion	Outcome (Positive + Neutral 0 Negative –)
3/20/95	Lori interrupts me on the phone.	I'm on the phone. Watch TV while you wait.	I don't want to watch TV.	I'll talk to you when I get off the phone!	– My child and I are both angry.

In the Kitchen

❧

ICPS WORD PAIRS: SET 1

IS/IS NOT   AND/OR   SAME/DIFFERENT
SOME/ALL   BEFORE/AFTER   NOW/LATER

In this room we focus on a set of carefully chosen vocabulary words, called ICPS Words, to help set the stage for children to later think about how to solve problems that arise with people.

In the Parent's Pages, you'll get a chance to take a close look at the way you talk with your children in conflict situations, and you'll see how using ICPS Words can help you begin the process of problem solving with your children.

Purpose

To use ICPS Words to help set the stage for later problem-solving thinking. By playing with these words in fun ways not associated with problem situations, your children will enjoy connecting them later in ways that will help them think about their problems. They'll learn, for example, to think that there are DIFFERENT ways to solve the SAME problem. They'll evaluate whether their idea IS or IS NOT a good one. These words can also help children learn to wait: "You can NOT go outside NOW. You can go outside LATER," and "Can you think of something DIFFERENT to do NOW while you wait?"

Materials Needed

Crayons. *For the first part of this activity, place a yellow and a green crayon on the table.*

Directions

Use figure 1. Emphasize the ICPS Words (in capital letters) with your voice. Point to each object and ask your child to name it. Tell your child the correct name, if needed. Some younger children may not know colors by name or the names of all the pictures. Nor is it important that they color within the lines. As you ask each question, they can just point to the pictures and answer those questions that they're able to.

In this and all games and activities to follow, read the Parent Script to your child.

Parent Script

Introduction of ICPS Games to Your Child

We're going to play some games called ICPS. ICPS means I Can Problem Solve. You're going to be able to think about what to do when you want something, or when you feel mad about something, or when you have to wait for what you want.

Even if you're already very good at solving problems, you can get even better. You'll get the idea as we go along. Now we're going to play a game with words that will help you solve problems later. Are you ready?

(Give your child a crayon and say:)

First we're going to play with some words. The first word is SAME.

Circle two foods that are the SAME.

Circle two foods that are DIFFERENT.

(Point to lettuce and beans.) Color these the color they really are when you see them.

How are lettuce *(point)* AND beans *(point)* the SAME?

How are they DIFFERENT?

Is corn *(point)* yellow OR is corn green?

Color the food that IS corn.

How is corn DIFFERENT from lettuce AND beans?

Color a food that is NOT lettuce.

Color ALL the things you can eat.

Circle SOME of the things you can NOT eat.

Circle ALL of the things you can NOT eat.

(Make up some questions using the ICPS Words.)

Fig. 1

(Use figure 2.)

What does this side of the table have *(point)* that this side *(point)* does NOT have?

OUR KITCHEN

Fig. 2

When you are actually in your kitchen, the questions below will help make learning the ICPS word pairs lively and engaging.

Parent Script

Let's play with some words again.

Do we get water from the sink OR from the stove?

Do we cook on the stove OR in the sink?

Do we cook in the kitchen OR in the bathroom?

Do we cook BEFORE or AFTER we go to bed?

Do I turn the stove off BEFORE or AFTER I finish cooking?

Are we cooking NOW or will I cook LATER?

What do we do in the kitchen that we do NOT do in the bedroom?

What can we do in the kitchen that is the SAME as we do in the living room?

What can we do in the kitchen that is DIFFERENT from what we do in the living room?

Are you emphasizing the ICPS Words (in capital letters)?

AT OUR DINNER TABLE (KITCHEN OR DINING ROOM)

Directions

Try using ICPS word pairs when you are together with your children at the dinner table.

Parent Script

Are we eating in the kitchen OR in the dining room?

I want you to point to something that IS (chicken, hamburger, etc.).

Now point to something that is DIFFERENT from (chicken, hamburger, etc.).

Point to two things on the table that are the SAME.

Point to a spoon AND a fork.

(Pick up a salt shaker.) Is this a salt shaker or NOT a salt shaker?

Point to the salt shaker AND a glass, but NOT a spoon.

Can you think of something we eat that is NOT on the table NOW?

What did you do BEFORE dinner?

What did you do AFTER school but BEFORE dinner?

Using ICPS Words, make up new questions of your own. You can now begin using the ICPS word pair posters in the back of this workbook, if you wish.

ICPS WORD PAIRS: SET 2

SOME OF THE TIME/ALL OF THE TIME
AT THE SAME TIME/NOT THE SAME TIME

Purpose

To help children later (1) appreciate that some solutions to problems will be successful "some of the time" but not "all of the time," and (2) recognize that some times are better than others to ask for something ("Mom cannot talk on the phone and talk to me at the same time").

Parent Script

Do we eat ALL OF THE TIME or SOME OF THE TIME?

Do we eat in the kitchen (dining room) ALL OF THE TIME or SOME OF THE TIME?

What else do you do in the kitchen SOME OF THE TIME, NOT ALL OF THE TIME?

What do I do in the kitchen SOME OF THE TIME?

Do I cook ALL OF THE TIME or SOME OF THE TIME?

Can we eat AND drink water AT THE SAME TIME?

Can we sit at the table AND eat at the SAME TIME?

What else can we do AT THE SAME TIME that we eat?

What else can we NOT do AT THE SAME TIME that we eat?

SEQUENCING

Purpose

To give children practice in using the words *BEFORE* and *AFTER* to help them later think about consequences ("I hit him before he hit me," "He hit me after I hit him").

Directions

Look at figure 3. The frames are not in the correct order. Ask your children to point to each picture as you ask the questions. Option: Duplicate this page, cut out each picture, and let your children place them in order as you ask each question.

Parent Script

What happens first? Which picture shows what happens first?

Then what?

What happens next?

Did the family eat AFTER the girl set the table?

Did the kids take the dishes off the table BEFORE or AFTER the family ate?

What MIGHT have happened BEFORE the girl set the table? Just make it up.

What might have happened AFTER the kids cleared the table? Just make it up.

Fig. 3

MY CHILD'S IDEAS:

IN OUR KITCHEN OR AT THE DINNER TABLE

Purpose

To give your children practice in building a problem-solving vocabulary.

Directions

When you are actually in your kitchen or at your dinner table, ask your child for ways to use the words you have been playing with so far. For example, you can point to a toaster and ask, "Can you think of a way to use the word NOT?" (If needed:) "This IS a toaster. It is NOT a (child answers)." Then ask your child to look around the kitchen and think of other ways to use the word NOT. You can use just one word or phrase, or use the word pair in one sentence, e.g., "Are a toaster and a stove the SAME or DIFFERENT?" "Are we at the dinner table SOME OF THE TIME or ALL OF THE TIME?" Continue with the other ICPS Words anytime you are in the kitchen or are eating together.

Record your child's ideas on the lines provided on the next page. It is very reinforcing for a child to see a parent record his or her ideas.

MY CHILD'S IDEAS WORKSHEET

DATE _____

Directions: Date this page as a way to log your child's progress.

IS/IS NOT _____
_____

AND/OR _____
_____

SAME/DIFFERENT _____
_____

SOME/ALL _____
_____

BEFORE/AFTER _____
_____

NOW/LATER _____
_____

ALL OF THE TIME/ _____
SOME OF THE TIME _____

TWO THINGS AT THE _____
SAME TIME _____

ICPS WORD PAIRS: SET 3

MIGHT/MAYBE   WHY/BECAUSE
GOOD TIME/NOT A GOOD TIME   GOOD PLACE/NOT A GOOD PLACE
GOOD IDEA/NOT A GOOD IDEA

Purpose

To help children begin thinking about consequences to acts, and to learn that timing is an important part of problem solving.

Directions

Point to each picture shown as you ask the corresponding questions.

Parent Script

A Glass Is on the Edge of the Table

(Point to figure 4a.)

Is this a GOOD PLACE for the glass?

If the glass is there, then what MIGHT happen next?

(If needed:) What else MIGHT happen?

Where IS a GOOD PLACE for the glass?

Fig. 4a

Child Is Helping with the Dishes

(Point to figure 4b.)

What is happening in this picture?

Is that a GOOD IDEA?

WHY IS that (is that NOT)
a GOOD IDEA? BECAUSE . . .

Fig. 4b

Child Sticks His Hand in the Egg Beater

(Point to figure 4c.)

What is happening in this picture?

Is that a GOOD PLACE for this child's hand?

What MIGHT happen if his hand is there?

Would that happen BEFORE or AFTER
he put his hand there?

Where is a GOOD PLACE for his hand?

Fig. 4c

Child Wants Mom to Read Her a Story While Mom Is Making Dinner

(Point to figure 4d.)

What is happening in this picture?

Can Mom cook dinner AND read the girl a story AT THE SAME TIME?

Is this A GOOD TIME or NOT A GOOD TIME for this girl to ask Mom to read her a story?

When IS A GOOD TIME to ask her?

If she asks at a NOT GOOD TIME, then what MIGHT happen next?

Fig. 4d

PARENT AND CHILD EXCHANGE

At this point we are looking at the annoying, everyday problem behaviors common with most children. The examples in this section are but a few of the ways in which children's behavior causes parents frustration.

Purpose

To help you think about particular behaviors that upset you, and to help you be prepared ahead of time with an ICPS response to those behaviors. This kind of readiness will help to prevent common, recurring problems from triggering a power struggle with your children.

It will be helpful to write down a typical exchange between you and your child when a problem comes up. For example, a child climbs up on top of a cabinet to get a cookie. With safety as the issue, the example below shows the exchange between a mother and her four-year-old *before* the mother learned ICPS.

Problem

Amy is climbing for cookies again.

Parent: Get down from there right now!

Child: I want a cookie.

Parent: How many times do I have to tell you not to climb?

Child: (pouts)

Parent: You're going to fall and hurt yourself.

Child: No, I won't.

Parent: Ask me if you want a cookie.

Child: OK.

Is this exchange a monologue or a dialogue? How we talk to or with children can be represented by four rungs of a ladder. Each rung of the ladder represents a different *style* of talking with children or way of handling a problem.

RUNG 1, at the bottom of the ladder, is called "Commands, Demands, Belittles, Punishes," a style of talk that tells children what to do in a negative, powerful way. *Example: "Get down from there right now!" or "Do you want a spanking?"*

RUNG 2 is called "Suggestions Without Explanation," a less negative style of talk that tells children what to do but does not tell them *why* they should do it. *Example: "Ask me if you want a cookie."*

RUNG 3 is called "Suggestions with Explanation, Including Feelings." While this style does explain why a child should or should not do something, and might include how you or someone else feels, it is still doing the thinking for the child. *Example: "I'll feel sad if you fall and hurt yourself."*

RUNG 4 takes explaining and reasoning one step further. It is called "ICPS Dialoguing: The Problem-Solving Process." When you are on RUNG 4, you are asking, not telling, your children what they should do, and why. *Example: "What MIGHT happen if you climb on top of the cabinet like that? How will I (you) feel if that happens?"*

We call our ladder the ICPS Dialogue Ladder because we want to climb to RUNG 4, the top of the ladder, to *two-way* conversations. I call these conversations ICPS Dialoguing, and it is the process by which parents help their children learn to think of their own and others' feelings, solutions, and consequences to acts.

To show you how to use the ladder, look at the sample on the next page and see where on the ladder the statements by this mother fall. Notice how the statements that best match this mother's are checked off. Also notice that everything this mother said is not shown on the ladder. You will see an example of a statement filled in on the blank line of the rung that best fits the *style* of what this mother said to her child—RUNG 1.

SAMPLE ICPS DIALOGUE LADDER

Problem

Child climbing on top of cabinet for a cookie.

ICPS Dialoguing: The Problem-Solving Process

| | RUNG 4 |

_____ Is that a GOOD PLACE to climb?

_____ What MIGHT happen if you do that?

_____ How MIGHT I (you) feel if that happens?

_____ What can you do so that will NOT happen?

_____ _____

Suggestions with Explanation, Including Feelings

RUNG 3

__X__ You might fall.

_____ I (you) will feel sad if you get hurt.

_____ The cookie jar might fall and break.

_____ _____

Suggestions Without Explanation

RUNG 2

__X__ Ask me if you want a cookie.

_____ Don't climb up there like that.

_____ Stay away from the cookies.

_____ _____

Commands, Demands, Belittles, Punishes

RUNG 1

__X__ Get down right now!

_____ How stupid can you be?

_____ Do you want a spanking (etc.)? No TV tonight!

__X__ *How many times do I have to tell you . . .*

The statements in the sample exchange fall on RUNGS 1, 2, and 3, a common mixture of several styles of talk. To get you started, the first exercise will use the same example as the one above. Try to stay with the issue of safety as the reason you do not want your children to climb. Other reasons, such as sneaking behind your back to get the cookies or eating before dinner, are given on page 29.

Write, just like a movie script, what you and your child typically do or say when he or she climbs up on top of the cabinet for cookies. That is, write what you do or say, then write what your child does or says. If this problem or something similar has never occurred, just make up what you and your child might do or say should such a problem occur.

You do not need to use all the lines provided. They are only there if you need them. In all exercises where you write in this workbook, you do not have to use the same number of lines.

PARENT AND CHILD EXCHANGE

Problem

_____

I did (said): _____

_____

Child: _____

Parent: _____

_____

Child: _____

Parent: _____

_____

Child: _____

Parent: _____

_____

Child: _____

Which rung of the ladder are you on?

Compare the statements or questions that you just wrote with those on the ladder on the next page. Check off on that rung of the ladder each of the statements or questions that best match your own.

If there are any statements or questions from your exchange that are not shown on the ladder, write them in on the blank line on the RUNG that best fits the *style* of your statement or question.

THE ICPS DIALOGUE LADDER

ICPS Dialoguing: The Problem-Solving Process

_____ Is that a GOOD PLACE to climb?

_____ What MIGHT happen if you do that?

_____ How MIGHT I (you) feel if that happens?

_____ What can you do so that will NOT happen?

_____ _____

Suggestions with Explanation, Including Feelings

_____ You might fall.

_____ I (you) will feel sad if you get hurt.

_____ The cookie jar might fall and break.

_____ _____

Suggestions Without Explanation

_____ Ask me if you want a cookie.

_____ Don't climb up there like that.

_____ Stay away from the cookies.

_____ _____

Commands, Demands, Belittles, Punishes

_____ Get down right now!

_____ How stupid can you be!

_____ Do you want a spanking (etc.)?

_____ No TV tonight!

_____ _____

RUNG 4

RUNG 3

RUNG 2

RUNG 1

If you are frequently climbing on RUNG 1, then you are in a power struggle with your children.

RUNG I is the place where parents use commanding, demanding, belittling, and punishing to try to change children's behavior. This method of discipline makes children feel frustrated and helpless, leading to feelings of aggression and a need to take out those feelings on safer objects, such as other children at school, younger children, or pets. The reverse response, to retreat, can also occur; some children withdraw and become timid and fearful. Children who feel a sense of control and do not feel powerless feel good about themselves and have no need to act aggressively or withdraw.

The ICPS approach does not imply that you should never get angry with your children. Everyone yells at times and makes demands on their children. Not getting angry now and then would be unnatural, especially when a parent feels exasperated because other ways of talking fall on deaf ears. And children have to learn to cope with your emotions as a problem to be solved. But if RUNG 1 is the predominant form of discipline, your children cannot gain that important sense of control that they need to navigate successfully through life.

Let's move on so you can see how you can jump over RUNGS 2 and 3, discussed in the next two rooms, and leap right to the top, RUNG 4, ICPS Dialoguing.

Look back at the last ICPS Dialogue Ladder. Notice that RUNG 4 dialoguing has a total of four questions, four parts. The first part uses ICPS Words that you have already "played with."

The next part consists of *consequences*, shown on the ladder by the question, "What MIGHT happen if you do that?" The third part consists of *feelings*, shown by the question, "How MIGHT I (you) feel if that happens?" Finally, the children think of *alternative behaviors* or *solutions* to problems, as shown by the question, "What can you do so that will NOT happen?"

Sometimes you will need to ask all the questions on RUNG 4, and sometimes you will have to ask only some of them.

DISSECTING RUNG 4 OF THE ICPS LADDER

Focus: ICPS Words

To help you learn the full ICPS dialoguing process, it is easier to practice one part at a time. First, you'll focus on the ICPS Words that you have used up to now in non-problem-solving situations in fun ways with your children (e.g., "Can I eat AND drink water AT THE SAME TIME?"). The ability to use these words will allow your children to engage in a meaningful dialogue with you when a problem comes up, such as "Can I cook dinner AND read you a story AT THE SAME TIME?" Not all problems will begin with the same ICPS Words. You will develop a feel for how to begin your dialogues as you move through this workbook.

Read the examples of how ICPS Words and phrases are used in the problem situations below. Then add your own ideas for use of these or any ICPS Words from Sets 1, 2, or 3. Reminders:

Set 1:   IS/IS NOT   AND/OR   SAME/DIFFERENT
          SOME/ALL   BEFORE/AFTER   NOW/LATER

Set 2:   SOME OF THE TIME/ALL OF THE TIME
          AT THE SAME TIME/NOT THE SAME TIME

Set 3:   MIGHT/MAYBE   WHY/BECAUSE
          GOOD TIME/NOT A GOOD TIME
          GOOD PLACE/NOT A GOOD PLACE
          GOOD IDEA/NOT A GOOD IDEA

RUNG 4: ICPS DIALOGUING (Problem Situations)

Problem

You come into the kitchen and discover your child climbing on top of a cabinet for cookies (because you think he's sneaking behind your back to get them).

ICPS Words (Samples)

Can you think of a DIFFERENT way to tell me what you want?

WHY do you think I do NOT want you to have the cookies NOW?

(If the reason you don't want your child to have cookies now is because it is just before dinner, ICPS Words can be used as follows.)

Is right BEFORE dinner a GOOD TIME or NOT A GOOD TIME to eat cookies?

Can you think of something DIFFERENT to do BEFORE dinner?

(Add your own ideas for questions with ICPS Words.)

_____

_____

_____

_____

Problem

During dinner, your child is interrupting his sister while she is talking.

ICPS Words (Samples)

Are you listening to your sister or NOT listening?

Can we hear you if you AND your sister talk AT THE SAME TIME?

(Add your own ideas for questions with ICPS Words.)

_____

_____

_____

Problem

Your child throws food on the floor.

ICPS Words (Samples)

Is the floor a GOOD PLACE or NOT A GOOD PLACE for your food?

(Add your own ideas.)

_____

_____

_____

Problem

Your child is eating with his fingers.

ICPS Words (Samples)

Can you think of a DIFFERENT way to eat?

(Add your own ideas.)

_____

_____

_____

Problem

Your child wants you to read her a story while you are trying to make dinner.

(What can you think of to write? Hint: The ICPS Words GOOD TIME, AT THE SAME TIME, NOW, LATER are useful.)

_____

_____

_____

   The ICPS Dialogue Ladder that follows shows various styles of handling the problem. (Child wants mother to read him or her a story while she is trying to make dinner.) Did you write ICPS Words for this problem? RUNG 4 shows only ICPS Words, what the focus has been in this room.

   Check off on the ladder the ICPS Words you wrote that most closely match those on RUNG 4. On the blank line, add any words that you wrote that are not shown on the ladder.

   Statements of RUNGS 1, 2, and 3 are also shown on the ladder to highlight how they differ from the ICPS approach on RUNG 4.

   Think about how you might have talked to your child before, or may still if he or she actually interrupts you while you are busy. Check off any statements below RUNG 4 that would match, or would be similar to, any you would still use now. Write in any statements you might use, but are not shown, on the blank line of the rungs that best fit the style of your statements.

THE ICPS DIALOGUE LADDER

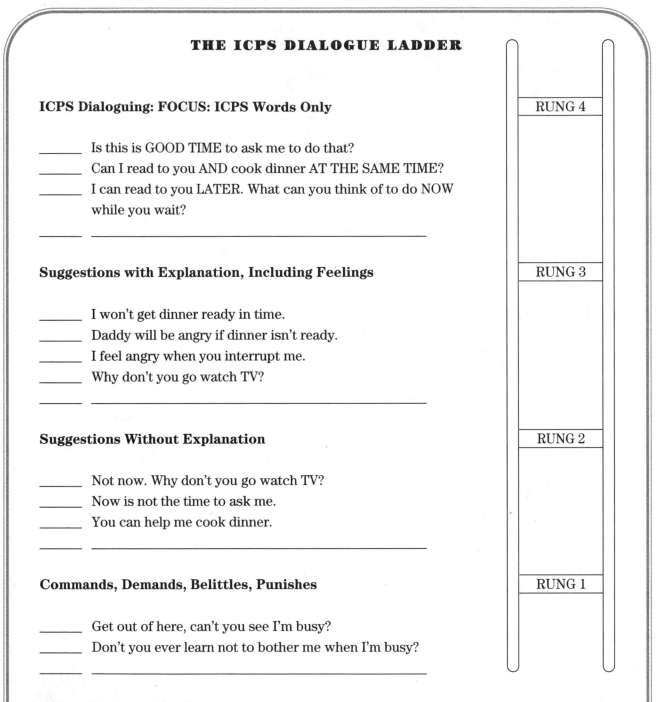

ICPS Dialoguing: FOCUS: ICPS Words Only

RUNG 4

_____ Is this is GOOD TIME to ask me to do that?
_____ Can I read to you AND cook dinner AT THE SAME TIME?
_____ I can read to you LATER. What can you think of to do NOW while you wait?

_____ _____

Suggestions with Explanation, Including Feelings

RUNG 3

_____ I won't get dinner ready in time.
_____ Daddy will be angry if dinner isn't ready.
_____ I feel angry when you interrupt me.
_____ Why don't you go watch TV?

_____ _____

Suggestions Without Explanation

RUNG 2

_____ Not now. Why don't you go watch TV?
_____ Now is not the time to ask me.
_____ You can help me cook dinner.

_____ _____

Commands, Demands, Belittles, Punishes

RUNG 1

_____ Get out of here, can't you see I'm busy?
_____ Don't you ever learn not to bother me when I'm busy?

_____ _____

Think of another problem between you and your child that often occurs in the kitchen or at the dinner table. Create your own questions that use ICPS Words.

In the next room, we will look more closely at RUNG 2, "Suggestions Without Explanation." We will then see how we can add another focus of RUNG 4, feeling words, to ICPS dialoguing.

In the Bedroom

❧

After playing with ICPS Words, games about people's *feelings* are added in this room.

In the Parent's Pages, you'll see how you can add feeling words to the ICPS Dialogue Ladder, and you'll look more closely at RUNG 2, "Suggestions Without Explanations."

First, a review of ICPS Words.

ICPS WORD PAIRS: SET 1

IS/IS NOT   AND/OR   SAME/DIFFERENT
SOME/ALL   BEFORE/AFTER   NOW/LATER

Purpose

By now your child will probably be able to use ICPS Words in everyday situations. By playing with these words here, your child will be able to generate his or her own ideas in this environment.

Games in this section also involve the need to listen and pay attention, skills important to solving problems with others.

Materials Needed

Crayons (any selection of colors)

Directions

Use figure 5. Ask your child to follow your directions. Go slowly. If your child is frustrated, stop and resume another time. This is supposed to be a fun time for both of you.

Fig. 5

Parent Script

Activities for ICPS Word Review

Color something that you do NOT wear.

Circle ALL the things that you do wear.

Color SOME of the things that you do wear.

Circle two things that are the SAME.

Color the dresser AND the bed, but NOT the window.

Did you color the dresser AND the bed the SAME color OR a DIFFERENT color?

Did you color the dresser BEFORE or AFTER you colored the bed?

Activities for Listening and Paying Attention

Now watch me carefully. I'm going to point to some pictures.

You have to remember what I point to.

(Point to the shirt.) Point to the SAME picture that I just did.

(Point to the shirt and the bed.) Now point to one thing that is the SAME AND one thing that is DIFFERENT from what I pointed to.

(Point to the shirt, the bed, the dresser, the socks, the toys.) Point to ALL of the things I just pointed to. Can you remember them?

Good, now point to SOME of the things, NOT ALL of the things, that I pointed to.

Now point to something I did NOT point to.

IN YOUR CHILD'S BEDROOM

Parent Script

(When you are actually in your child's bedroom, ask:)

You put socks in your dresser. What else do you put in your dresser?

What does NOT go in your dresser?

What else does NOT go in your dresser? You can be silly.

Does your bed go in your dresser?

No, your bed does NOT go in your dresser.

What room is your bed in?

What room is your bed NOT in?

Do you sleep in your bedroom OR in the bathroom?

Do you brush your teeth in the bedroom OR in the bathroom?

(Make up your own questions using these words. Continue as long as your child is interested.)

ICPS WORDS: SET 2

SOME OF THE TIME/ALL OF THE TIME
AT THE SAME TIME/NOT THE SAME TIME

Parent Script

Do you sleep AND eat (do your homework, etc.) AT THE SAME TIME?

Can you get into your pajamas and get into bed AT THE SAME TIME?

What else can you NOT do AT THE SAME TIME you sleep (do homework, etc.)?

Do you sleep ALL OF THE TIME or SOME OF THE TIME?

AT BEDTIME

Do you brush your teeth BEFORE or AFTER you get out of bed?

Do you put your toys away BEFORE or AFTER you go to bed?

What else do you do BEFORE you go to bed?

You *(repeat child's answer)* AND _____.

Do you sleep ALL OF THE TIME or SOME OF THE TIME?

WHILE DRESSING

Bring me your (white) socks, NOT your (blue) socks.

Put on your (blue) shirt (blouse) AND your (white) pants (skirt), but NOT your red pants.

WHILE DOING HOMEWORK (If Applicable)

Do you do your homework BEFORE or AFTER you watch TV?

Can you do your homework and sleep AT THE SAME TIME?

Directions

As in the kitchen/dinner table examples, ask your child for ways to use the ICPS Words in his or her bedroom. Record your child's ideas on the worksheet provided on the next page.

MY CHILD'S IDEAS WORKSHEET

DATE _____

Directions: Date this page as a way to log your child's progress.

IS/IS NOT
_____
_____

AND/OR
_____
_____

SAME/DIFFERENT
_____
_____

SOME/ALL
_____
_____

BEFORE/AFTER
_____
_____

NOW/LATER
_____
_____

ALL OF THE TIME/
SOME OF THE TIME
_____
_____

TWO THINGS AT THE
SAME TIME
_____
_____

FEELING WORDS

HAPPY   SAD   ANGRY   AFRAID   PROUD   FRUSTRATED
HOW DO THEY FEEL?

Purpose

To help children develop two skills important in problem solving: (1) a sensitivity to how people feel that makes it possible to think later about how a solution to a problem can affect one's own and another's feelings, and (2) a recognition that the SAME person can feel DIFFERENT ways at different times, which is important for timing. (A child can learn to think, "I will NOT ask her NOW, I will wait until she is in a better mood.")

Materials

Crayons (yellow, blue, red, purple, orange, green)

Directions

As you ask your child the questions below, make the feeling expressions along with him or her.

Parent Script

Today's ICPS game is about how people feel.

First, make a HAPPY face.

Now show me a SAD face.

What do you look like when you are MAD?

How about SCARED?

Can you look PROUD?

What about FRUSTRATED?

Directions

Use figure 6.

Color someone who is feeling HAPPY yellow.

Color someone who is feeling the SAME way yellow.

Color someone who is feeling SAD blue.

Color someone who is feeling ANGRY red.

Circle the SAME person who is feeling DIFFERENT ways.

Can the SAME person feel DIFFERENT ways at DIFFERENT times?

Do I feel the SAME way ALL OF THE TIME?

I feel HAPPY SOME OF THE TIME. I do NOT feel HAPPY ALL OF THE TIME.

Point to someone who is NOT feeling HAPPY.

Point to a girl who is feeling HAPPY, NOT who is feeling SAD.

Color someone who is feeling AFRAID.

Color someone who is feeling PROUD.

Point to the father AND to the boy who are feeling PROUD.

Color someone who is feeling FRUSTRATED.

Point to ALL the people who are feeling PROUD or HAPPY.

Point to SOME of the people who are NOT feeling SAD.

Point to ALL of the people who are NOT feeling SAD.

(Make up some more questions like these, and let your child make up some too.)

HOW DO WE FEEL ABOUT THIS?

Purpose

To help you appreciate your child's feelings about things, and to help your child appreciate that you have feelings too.

Materials

Crayons (yellow, blue, red, green)

Fig. 6

Directions

Point to each figure below as you ask the corresponding questions.

The colors represent feelings. For younger children, you may wish to use only yellow (happy), blue (sad), and red (angry, mad). For children ages five and older, add green (frustrated).

Parent Script

Girl's Shoelace Broke

Today's ICPS game is about how we feel about things.

(Point to figure 7a.)

What is happening in this picture?

Fig. 7a

HAPPY   SAD   ANGRY   FRUSTRATED

Here's how we'll play this game. I'm going to guess how you would feel if that happened to you. AFTER I close my eyes, you color the square next to the picture *(point to the square)*. Listen carefully.

If this would make you HAPPY, color it yellow.

(Point to appropriate feeling faces at the bottom of page 42.)

If this would make you SAD, color it blue.

If this would make you ANGRY, color it red.

If this would make you FRUSTRATED, color it green.

OK. What color is HAPPY? SAD? ANGRY? FRUSTRATED? *(Let child answer.)*

I'm going to close my eyes now. Color the square. Tell me when you're finished coloring the square.

(With your eyes still closed:) I guess that you colored it (green) because that would make you feel (FRUSTRATED).

(Open your eyes now.) (If you guessed correctly): Oh, I guessed how you'd feel.

Do you think I would feel the SAME way or a DIFFERENT way if that happened to me?

(Let child answer.)

Yes, I would feel the SAME way about that.

(If you did not guess): Oh, I did NOT guess how you'd feel.

WHY would you feel that way?

Child Is Sick in Bed

(Point to figure 7b.)

What is happening in this picture?

Next to this picture there are two squares because we're both going to color one of them.

First, we'll do what we did before.

You color a square that shows how you would feel if you were sick in bed, and I'm going to guess how it would make you feel.

Remember, yellow is for HAPPY. *(Repeat colors and their feeling words as needed.)*

I'm going to close my eyes now. Tell me when you're finished coloring the square.

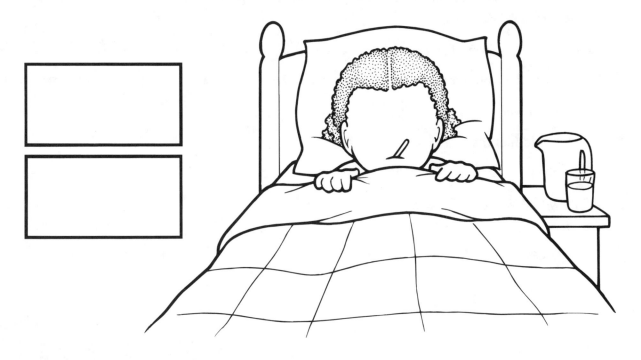

Fig. 7b

HAPPY   SAD   ANGRY   FRUSTRATED

(With your eyes still closed) I guess you colored it blue because that would make you feel sad.

(Open your eyes.) Oh, I did guess (did NOT guess) how you'd feel.

(If did not guess): WHY would you feel that way?

Now we're going to change the game.

You close your eyes and guess how it would make me feel if you were sick in bed.

(Make sure your child's eyes are closed. Color the square.) OK, keep your eyes closed. Guess what color I colored the square to show how I would feel about this.

(Let child guess.) You can open your eyes now.

Oh, you did (did NOT) guess.

Would we feel the SAME way or a DIFFERENT way about this?

(If different): You said *you* would be (HAPPY) to be sick in bed. Can you tell me WHY *I* would feel (SAD)?

Do we always feel the SAME way about the SAME thing?

Child's Room Is Messy

(Point to figure 7c.)

What is happening in this picture?

We're both going to color a square again.

You color a square that shows how you would feel if your room were messy. I'm going to guess how it would make you feel.

Fig. 7c

HAPPY   SAD   ANGRY   FRUSTRATED

Remember, yellow is for HAPPY. *(Repeat colors and their feeling words as needed.)*

I'm going to close my eyes now. Tell me when you're finished coloring the square.

(With your eyes still closed): I guess you colored it blue because that would make you feel SAD.

(Open your eyes.) Oh, I did guess (did NOT guess) how you'd feel.

(If did not guess): WHY would you feel that way?

Now you close your eyes and guess how it would make *me* feel if your room were messy.

(Make sure your child's eyes are closed. Color the square.) OK, keep your eyes closed. Guess what color I colored the square to show how I would feel about this.

(Let child guess.) You can open your eyes now.

Oh, you did (did NOT) guess.

Would we feel the SAME way or a DIFFERENT way about this?

(If different): You said *you* would feel (HAPPY) if your room were messy. Can you tell me WHY *I* would feel (ANGRY)?

Note: When you ask children why they feel a way about something, you may learn something important about how they think.

What else can happen in your bedroom that makes you feel:

HAPPY? _____

SAD? _____

ANGRY? _____

FRUSTRATED? _____

How about:

PROUD? _____

AFRAID? _____

Are there any other things that happen or MIGHT happen in your bedroom that you have feelings about? *(If needed):* "How does that make you feel?"

Note: Teaching children to recognize feelings is an important element in guiding their behavior. Even very young children can learn to understand and correctly label their own feelings, and by age four or five, they are more able to recognize the feelings of others.

Whether your children are boys or girls, it is critical that they express their own feelings accurately and that they be able to demonstrate those feelings in words, such as "That makes me mad." If you are sensitive and empathize with your children's feelings, then your children will likely develop a sensitivity ("empathy") for others.

Try to guide your children away from consequences that merely avoid punishment, such as "Mom will make me pick up the toys" or "Mom will send me to my room." By asking, "What else might happen?" you might eventually hear "Someone might trip over them." The implication is that your children will feel bad if someone gets hurt.

At this point your children are beginning to identify cause-and-effect relationships. They will come to understand that their own choice of behaviors will cause responses in others, and they will become more skilled at choosing strategies with less negative consequences.

ICPS WORD PAIRS: SET 3

MIGHT/MAYBE   WHY/BECAUSE
GOOD TIME/NOT A GOOD TIME   GOOD PLACE/NOT A GOOD PLACE
GOOD IDEA/NOT A GOOD IDEA

Directions

Point to each picture below as you ask the corresponding questions. Your child can point to the feeling faces.

Parent Script

Child Is Getting Dressed, Not Dawdling

(Point to figure 8a.)

What is happening in this picture? *(Tell child if needed.)*

Is that a GOOD IDEA?

WHY is that a GOOD IDEA? BECAUSE _____.

How MIGHT his mom (dad) feel when he does that?

Fig. 8a

HAPPY   SAD   ANGRY   AFRAID   PROUD   FRUSTRATED

Child Is Reading a Book After Bedtime

(Point to figure 8b.)

What is happening in this picture. *(Tell child if needed.)*

Is this a GOOD TIME or NOT A GOOD TIME to look at a book?

If this child looks at a book AFTER bedtime,
then what MIGHT happen next?

How MIGHT he feel if that happens?

When IS a GOOD TIME to look at a book?

Fig. 8b

HAPPY   SAD   ANGRY   AFRAID   PROUD   FRUSTRATED

Fig. 8c

HAPPY　　SAD　　ANGRY　　AFRAID　　PROUD　　FRUSTRATED

Child Is Going to Bed on Time

(Point to figure 8c.)

What is happening in this picture? *(Tell child if needed.)*

Is it a GOOD IDEA or NOT A GOOD IDEA to go to bed on time?

If she does NOT go to bed on time, what MIGHT happen?

How MIGHT she feel if that happens?

Fig. 8d

 HAPPY   SAD    ANGRY    AFRAID   PROUD   FRUSTRATED

Child Is Throwing Toys All Over the Floor

(Point to figure 8d.)

What is happening in this picture? *(Tell child if needed.)*

Is this a GOOD IDEA or NOT A GOOD IDEA?

If her toys are all over the floor, then what MIGHT HAPPEN next?

How MIGHT she feel if that happens?

How do you think her mom (dad) MIGHT feel if that happens?

Can you think of something DIFFERENT to do with your toys so those things won't happen and people won't feel that way?

PARENT AND CHILD EXCHANGE

Write what you and your child typically do or say when your child is having a problem with you or another adult. That is, write what you do or say, then write what your child does or says.

Problem

Your child won't go to bed on time. If this problem has never occurred, just make up what you and your child might do or say should such a problem occur.

I did (said): _____

_____

Child: _____

Parent: _____

_____

Child: _____

Parent: _____

_____

Child: _____

Parent: _____

_____

Child: _____

Is this exchange a monologue or a dialogue? Which rung of the ICPS Dialogue Ladder are you on now? On each rung, check off those statements that best match your own. As you did in the first room, write any response not already on the ladder on the blank line within the rung that best fits the *style* of your response.

THE ICPS DIALOGUE LADDER

ICPS Dialoguing: The Problem-Solving Process

_____ Is this a GOOD TIME to read (watch a video)?

_____ What MIGHT happen if you do that?

_____ How MIGHT I (you) feel tomorrow if that happens?

_____ What can you do so that will NOT happen?

_____ *(or, if next morning)* Are you tired OR NOT tired NOW?

_____ What can you do tonight so you will NOT be tired?

_____ _____

Suggestions with Explanation, Including Feelings

_____ Your (sister) is older, she can stay up later.

_____ You'll be tired in the morning.

_____ I'll feel sad if you get sick.

_____ _____

Suggestions Without Explanation

_____ It's time to go to bed.

_____ Watch your video earlier.

_____ _____

Commands, Demands, Belittles, Punishes

_____ I said, go to bed now!

_____ How many times have I told you . . . ?

_____ How stupid can you be?

_____ You can't watch the video at all!

_____ _____

RUNG 4

RUNG 3

RUNG 2

RUNG 1

If you find you are on RUNG 2, you may still be in a power struggle, although less angry in tone than on RUNG 1. Or you may feel that you have to tell your child what to do. However, he or she is still not engaged in the thinking process.

Let's move on so you can see how you can jump over RUNG 3 and leap right onto RUNG 4, ICPS Dialoguing.

DISSECTING RUNG 4 OF THE ICPS LADDER

Focus: ICPS Words and Feelings

As you did in the kitchen and at the dinner table, you can begin in the bedroom with ICPS Words that you have used in fun ways with your child, such as "Are you getting dressed NOW OR NOT getting dressed NOW?" For the problems below, we will now add the use of *feeling* words. You can use any feeling words. As a reminder, we have used HAPPY, SAD, MAD (ANGRY), AFRAID (SCARED), PROUD, and FRUSTRATED.

On the blank lines, fill in ways to use ICPS Words and Feelings in the problem situations described below.

Problem

Your child is drawing on the wall.

ICPS Words (Samples)

Is this a GOOD PLACE or NOT A GOOD PLACE to draw?

Where IS a good place to draw?

(Add your own ideas for questions with ICPS Words.)

_____

_____

_____

Sample Dialogue If Child Says "Good Place"

Parent: WHY do you think this IS a good place?

Child: I don't have any paper.

Parent: How could you find out how to get paper?

Add Feelings

How do you think I feel when you draw on wall and NOT on paper? *(If needed)*: HAPPY OR ANGRY?

How do *you* feel about the way the wall looks?

Do you and I feel the SAME way OR a DIFFERENT way about this?

(Add your own ideas for questions using Feeling words.)

_____

_____

_____

Problem

Your child is climbing on dresser.

ICPS Words (Samples)

Is this (your dresser) a GOOD PLACE to climb?

WHY do you think that?

(Add your own ideas.)

_____

_____

_____

Add Feelings

How do you think I feel when you climb in a NOT GOOD PLACE?

(Add your own ideas.)

_____

_____

_____

Problem

Your child is dressing too slowly, dawdling.

ICPS Words (Samples)

Are you thinking about getting dressed OR about something else?

If you dress so slowly, then will (we be late to Grandma's OR NOT late to Grandma's)?

(Add your own ideas.)

_____

_____

_____

Add Feelings

How do you think I feel when you dress so slowly?

How will (Grandma feel if we are late for the dinner she is cooking for us)?

(Add your own ideas.)

_____

_____

_____

HINT: If your child is carrying on, having a temper tantrum, or otherwise talking to you in ways you do not appreciate, one simple sentence can be used that both includes an ICPS Word and shows an interest in your child's feelings.

    You can ask, "Can you think of a DIFFERENT way to tell me how you feel?"

Problem

Your Child Won't Clean His/Her Room.

What can you think of to write? Think of questions that include ICPS Words and how both you and your child might feel.

ICPS Words

_____

_____

_____

Feelings

_____

_____

_____

The ICPS Ladder that follows shows various styles of handling this last problem.

RUNG 4 shows only what the focus has been in this room: ICPS Words and Feelings.

Compare the questions you just wrote using ICPS Words and Feelings with those on RUNG 4 and check off those that most closely match. On the blank line, add any you wrote that are not shown on the ladder.

Statements of RUNGS 1, 2, and 3 are also shown on the ladder to highlight how they differ from the ICPS approach on RUNG 4.

Check off any statements that would match or would be similar to any you might still use should your child actually not want to clean his or her room. Write in any statements you might use, and that are not shown, on the blank line of the rung that best fits the *style* of those statements.

THE ICPS DIALOGUE LADDER

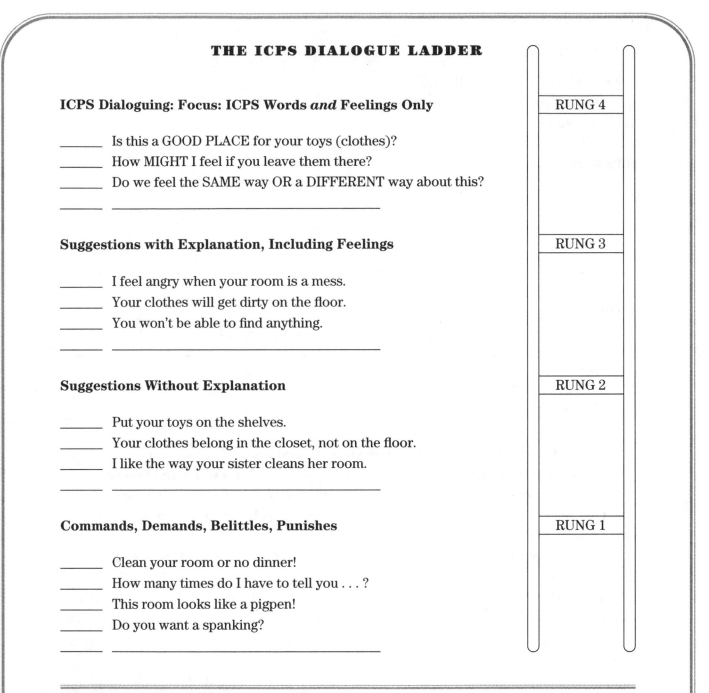

ICPS Dialoguing: Focus: ICPS Words *and* Feelings Only

RUNG 4

_____ Is this a GOOD PLACE for your toys (clothes)?
_____ How MIGHT I feel if you leave them there?
_____ Do we feel the SAME way OR a DIFFERENT way about this?
_____ _____

Suggestions with Explanation, Including Feelings

RUNG 3

_____ I feel angry when your room is a mess.
_____ Your clothes will get dirty on the floor.
_____ You won't be able to find anything.
_____ _____

Suggestions Without Explanation

RUNG 2

_____ Put your toys on the shelves.
_____ Your clothes belong in the closet, not on the floor.
_____ I like the way your sister cleans her room.
_____ _____

Commands, Demands, Belittles, Punishes

RUNG 1

_____ Clean your room or no dinner!
_____ How many times do I have to tell you . . . ?
_____ This room looks like a pigpen!
_____ Do you want a spanking?
_____ _____

Note: One goal in having children clean their rooms is to teach them responsibility. If you are not really concerned about which shelves the toys go on, or in which drawer the socks go, let your children take pride in making those decisions themselves. You can say, "You decide on which shelf to put your truck." In this way, your children are engaged in the thinking process yet behave in ways consistent with your style of childrearing.

Visit the next room and we will look more closely at RUNG 3, "Suggestions with Explanations, including Feelings." We will also see examples of how we can add a new focus of RUNG 4, "Solutions," to solve a problem.

In the Bathroom

❧

In this room, solutions—thinking that there is more than one way to solve problems—are added to ICPS Words and Feelings.

In the Parent's Pages, you'll see examples of how you can add questions to help your child think of solutions in various kinds of situations. You'll also look more closely at RUNG 3 of the ICPS Dialogue Ladder, "Suggestions with Explanations."

First, a review of ICPS words.

ICPS WORD PAIRS: SET I

IS/IS NOT   AND/OR   SAME/DIFFERENT
SOME/ALL   BEFORE/AFTER   NOW/LATER

I have included ICPS Words here for review if needed. If your child is using these words with success, feel free to skip this review.

Materials

Crayons (any colors)

Directions

Use figure 10.

Fig. 10

Parent Script

Do you brush your teeth in the bathtub OR in the sink?

Do you dry yourself with water OR with a towel?

How are the sink AND the bathtub DIFFERENT?

How are the sink AND the bathtub the SAME?

How are the sink, the toilet, AND the bathtub the SAME?

What is true about the sink that is NOT true about the toilet?

Circle ALL of the towels.

Color SOME of the towels blue *(let child choose color)*.

Choose a towel that you did NOT color, and color it a DIFFERENT color NOW.

Tell me something you do NOT do in the bath (shower).

What else do you NOT do in the bath (shower)?

Now listen carefully. This is a little harder. I am thinking of something in our (your) bathroom. See if you can tell me what it is.

I am NOT thinking of something in your (our) bathroom that IS yellow (a yellow towel, etc.).

I am NOT thinking of the _____ (yellow towel).

I am thinking of something that has water.

I am thinking of something that has water that you can NOT sit in OR on.

What am I NOT thinking of?

What else am I NOT thinking of?

I am thinking of something that has water AND that you can brush your teeth in.

What am I thinking of?

What else can you do in the sink? You can brush your teeth AND you can _____.

ICPS WORD PAIRS: SET 2

SOME OF THE TIME/ALL OF THE TIME
AT THE SAME TIME/NOT AT THE SAME TIME

Parent Script

Do we brush our teeth ALL OF THE TIME or SOME OF THE TIME?

Are you in the bathroom SOME OF THE TIME or ALL OF THE TIME?

WHILE BATHING

(While child is taking bath): Are you taking a bath NOW or NOT NOW?

Will you dry yourself BEFORE or AFTER you get out of the tub?

What else will you do AFTER you get out of the tub?

What will you do BEFORE you get out of the tub?

Can you take a bath and brush your teeth AT THE SAME TIME?

What else can you NOT do AT THE SAME TIME you take a bath?

Can you take a bath AND sing AT THE SAME TIME?

What else can you do AT THE SAME TIME you take a bath?

Directions

Ask your child for ways to use the ICPS Words in the bathroom, and record his or her ideas on the next page.

MY CHILD'S IDEAS WORKSHEET

DATE _____

Directions: Date this page as a way to log your child's progress.

IS/IS NOT _____
_____

AND/OR _____
_____

SAME/DIFFERENT _____
_____

SOME/ALL _____
_____

BEFORE/AFTER _____
_____

NOW/LATER _____
_____

ALL OF THE TIME/ _____
SOME OF THE TIME _____

TWO THINGS AT THE _____
SAME TIME _____

ICPS WORD PAIRS: SET 3

MIGHT/MAYBE   WHY/BECAUSE
GOOD TIME/NOT A GOOD TIME   GOOD PLACE/NOT A GOOD PLACE
GOOD IDEA/NOT A GOOD IDEA

Directions

Point to the pictures below and ask the following questions. Your children may point to the feeling faces.

Parent Script

Child Is in the Bathtub with Her Clothes On

(Point to figure 11a.)

What is happening in this picture?

Is this a GOOD PLACE or NOT A GOOD PLACE to wear clothes?

If she does that, then what MIGHT happen?

How MIGHT she feel if that happens?

How MIGHT her mom (dad) feel if that happens?

Where IS a GOOD PLACE to wear her clothes?

Fig. 11a

Child Is Brushing Teeth

(Point to figure 11b.)

What is happening in this picture?

Is it a GOOD IDEA or NOT A GOOD IDEA to brush his teeth?

WHY IS that a GOOD IDEA? BECAUSE _____. (Let child answer.)

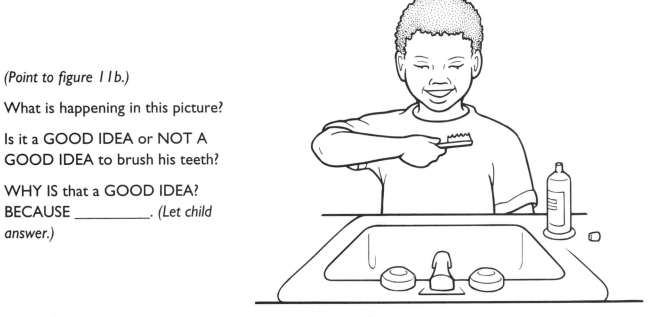

Fig. 11b

Child Is Drying Herself After Getting Out of the Tub

(Point to figure 11c.)

What is happening in this picture?

Is she drying herself BEFORE or AFTER her bath?

Is it a GOOD TIME to dry herself BEFORE OR AFTER she gets out of the tub?

WHY is it NOT A GOOD TIME to dry herself BEFORE she gets out of the bath?

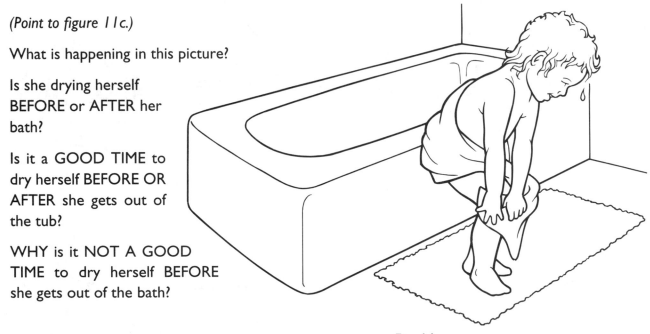

Fig. 11c

Child Is Throwing Toys out of the Bathtub

(Point to figure 11d.)

What is happening in this picture?

Is this a GOOD IDEA or NOT A GOOD IDEA?

WHY is this *(repeat child's answer)*. BECAUSE _____. *(Let child answer.)*

If his toys are all over the floor, then what MIGHT happen next?

Hint: Try to encourage consequences such as "someone might trip on them." If your child states a punishment, such as "Mom will get mad," ask "What else MIGHT happen?"

How MIGHT he feel if that happens?

How do you think his mom (dad) MIGHT feel if that happens?

Can you think of a DIFFERENT place (a good place) for his toys so that will NOT happen?

What can he do with his toys that is DIFFERENT from throwing them out of the bathtub?

Fig. 11d

WHAT ELSE CAN I DO?

ADD SOLUTIONS

Purpose

To focus on thinking of solutions, which in parent/child problem situations can mean more than one way to do things, more than one place to put things, and more than one time to ask for something. Thinking in this way not only reduces tension between a parent and a child—for example, when the child is throwing water on the floor in the bathroom—but it also is an important precursor to thinking of alternative solutions to any problem that comes up between people. A child can later think, for example, "If one idea doesn't work, I can try a DIFFERENT way."

Parent Script

There's more than one thing you can do with water.

You can drink water.

What else can you do with water? Try to think of lots of DIFFERENT things you can do with water.

You can drink water AND _____.

AND _____.

You've thought of two things you can do with water *(show two fingers)*.

Can you think of a third thing *(show three fingers)*?

(Continue until your child runs out of ideas.)

Note: If your child says, "Wash my face" and "Wash my hands," that is what we call an enumeration, or two variations of the same theme. In response, you should say, "Those are kind of the SAME because they are both washing something." Then ask, "Can you think of something DIFFERENT from washing something?"

PARENT AND CHILD EXCHANGE

Write what you do or say when your child is having a problem with you or another adult—that is, what you and your child typically do or say.

Sample Problems (Potential Harm)

1. Your child is jumping in the bathtub.
2. Your child is letting the water overflow in the sink.

If these problems have never occurred, just make up what you and your child might do or say if one of them did occur.

Problem

_____

I did (said): _____

_____

Child: _____

Parent: _____

_____

Child: _____

Parent: _____

_____

Child: _____

Parent: _____

_____

Child: _____

Is this exchange a monologue or a dialogue? See which rung of the ICPS Dialogue Ladder you are on now by comparing your statements or questions with those on the next page. Check off on each rung of the ladder each of the statements that best matches your own, and write any others in the blank line of the rung that best fits the *style* of your statements.

THE ICPS DIALOGUE LADDER

ICPS Dialoguing: The Problem-Solving Process

_____ Is that a GOOD PLACE (GOOD IDEA) to jump (let water run over)?

_____ What MIGHT happen if you do that?

_____ How MIGHT I (you) feel if that happens?

_____ What can you do so that will NOT happen?

_____ _____

Suggestions with Explanation, Including Feelings

_____ You might fall (slip on the water).

_____ I (you) will feel very sad if you get hurt.

_____ Tubs (sinks) are for bathing.

_____ Running water costs money.

_____ _____

Suggestions Without Explanation

_____ Stand in the tub, don't jump.

_____ Don't let the water spill over onto the floor.

_____ Turn the water off, it's spilling over.

_____ _____

Commands, Demands, Belittles, Punishes

_____ Stop jumping (running water) like that!

_____ How many times have I told you . . . ?

_____ Turn that water off! I don't have time to clean this mess!

_____ _____

RUNG 4

RUNG 3

RUNG 2

RUNG 1

If you are *not* on RUNGS 1, 2, or 3, you are probably dialoguing the ICPS way.

If you are frequently on RUNG 3, then you are helping your child understand why she or he should or shouldn't do something, often including telling how you feel. But you are still doing the thinking for your child.

In the next room we will use all the parts on RUNG 4. For now, let's move on so you can see how you can leave RUNG 3 and continue to climb onto RUNG 4.

DISSECTING RUNG 4 OF THE ICPS DIALOGUE LADDER

Focus: ICPS Words, Feelings, and Alternatives

Alternatives include use of ICPS Words such as "I can think of a DIFFERENT time, place, or idea" and "I can do something so that I, and my mom and dad, will feel a DIFFERENT way."

As we have illustrated in exercises that take place in the kitchen, at the dinner table, and in your child's bedroom, you can begin in the bathroom by using the ICPS Words that you have used in other fun ways with them, such as "Can you take a bath and brush your teeth AT THE SAME TIME?" and "Should we let the water out BEFORE or AFTER we get out of the tub?"

In the bedroom exercises, we added the use of Feeling words—words that can also be used in the bathroom, such as, "How does drying yourself AFTER a bath make you feel?"

Add Solutions

Now we're going to add thinking about Solutions, or alternative ways to do things. In a non-interpersonal situation, your child has told you different (alternative) things he or she could do with water. Now your child is ready to think of alternative ways to solve a "people" problem. In the parent/child problems in this section, solutions usually involve such alternatives as a "different place, time, or idea."

On the blank lines provided, write in ways to use ICPS Words, Feelings, and Solutions (al-ternatives) in the problem situations described below.

Problem

Your child doesn't want to take a bath.

ICPS Words (Samples)

Can you tell me WHY you do NOT want to take a bath?

Is it a GOOD IDEA OR NOT a good idea to NOT take a bath?

(Add your own ideas for questions with ICPS Words.)

_____

_____

_____

Note: By asking children "why," in a nonthreatening tone, you might learn something about what is on their minds, which you most likely will not learn by using the techniques on RUNGS 1, 2, or 3.

Add Feelings

How do you think I feel when you will NOT take a bath? *(If needed):* HAPPY OR ANGRY (FRUSTRATED)?

How do *you* feel about NOT taking a bath?

Do you and I feel the SAME way OR a DIFFERENT way about this?

(Add your own ideas for questions using Feeling Words.)

_____

_____

_____

Add Solutions

Can you think of something DIFFERENT to do so I will NOT feel (ANGRY, FRUSTRATED)?

(or): Can you think of a DIFFERENT way to get clean, something DIFFERENT you can do?

(Child might think of sponging herself outside of the bathtub. When your child is allowed to have some control over the situation, she is more likely to participate in reaching the real goal, in this case, getting washed.)

(Add your own ideas on how to help child solve this problem.)

_____

_____

_____

Problem

Your (younger) child won't use the toilet, even though toilet trained.

ICPS Words (Samples)

Are (your pants) a GOOD PLACE OR NOT A GOOD PLACE to *(use the words you normally use for this problem).*

(If child says "NOT good place"): Where IS a GOOD PLACE TO _____?

(If child says "good place"): Why do you think that?

(Asking why, in a nonthreatening tone, might reveal information about what's on your child's mind that could be important, and form the basis for further dialogue.)

WHY do you NOT use the toilet? BECAUSE _____.

(Add your own ideas.)

_____

_____

_____

Add Feelings

How do you think I feel when you do NOT use the toilet?

How do *you* feel when you do NOT use the toilet?

Do we feel the SAME way about this OR a DIFFERENT way?

(Add your own ideas.)

_____

_____

_____

Add Solutions

Can you think of a DIFFERENT place to (_____) so Mommy (Daddy) will NOT feel (angry).

You thought of that all by yourself. How does that make you feel? *(If needed):* PROUD or SAD?

(If needed): What can Mommy (Daddy) do to help you go back to the toilet?

(Add your own ideas.)

_____

_____

_____

Note: Toilet training is often a complicated process and sometimes, after it seems to have been accomplished, children will regress. If you have ruled out any physical explanations, consider whether or not it is a response to a new baby or other potential stress, a reaction to a new food, etc.

Not using the toilet can also be a young child's way of maintaining some control. Think about how you handle situations with your children in general. If you are primarily on RUNGS 1 or 2, or even RUNG 3, your children may not feel listened to, and refusing to use the toilet may be their one way of gaining control over you. By asking your children RUNG 4 questions, you are sharing control with them, which is what they may be seeking in the first place.

If you fear giving your children control, think about this: When they refuse to use the toilet, have temper tantrums, etc., *who is in control?* In the end, you will gain control by giving your children control.

Problem

Your child won't get out of the bathroom when others are trying to get in (because he's dawdling). What can you think of to write? Think of questions that include ICPS Words, Feelings, Solutions.

ICPS Words

_____

_____

_____

Add Feelings

_____

_____

_____

Add Solutions

_____

_____

_____

Were you able to write ICPS Words, Feelings, and Solutions similar to those shown on RUNG 4 of the ladder that follows?

On the following ICPS Dialogue Ladder, check off any other statements you might use that most closely match those on various rungs on the ladder, and write any others on the blank line of the rung that best fits the *style* of your statement.

THE ICPS DIALOGUE LADDER

ICPS Dialoguing: Focus: ICPS Words, Feelings, and Solutions Only

_____ How MIGHT (another person) feel about that?

_____ What can you do so _____ will NOT feel that way?

_____ Can you think of a DIFFERENT place to (comb your hair)?

_____ _____

RUNG 4

Suggestions with Explanation, Including Feelings

_____ Your (sister) is angry, she needs the bathroom.

_____ When you dawdle in the bathroom, others can't get in.

_____ Someone could have an accident if you don't come out of there.

_____ _____

RUNG 3

Suggestions Without Explanation

_____ Please move a little faster in there.

_____ Read in your room, not in the bathroom.

_____ Be more considerate of others around here.

_____ _____

RUNG 2

Commands, Demands, Belittles, Punishes

_____ Get out of there now!

_____ How many times do I have to tell you . . . ?

_____ You're being very selfish.

_____ _____

RUNG 1

Record below any problem between you and your child that often occurs in the bathroom. Create your own use of ICPS Words, Feelings, and Solutions.

Problem

_____

_____

_____

ICPS Words

_____

_____

_____

Add Feelings

_____

_____

_____

Add Solutions

_____

_____

_____

You are now entering our last room in the house, the living room/family room, where you will focus on the final part of ICPS dialoguing on RUNG 4, that of thinking about consequences.

You will also practice all four parts of the ICPS dialogue process: (1) ICPS words, (2) Feelings, (3) Solutions, and (4) Consequences.

Are you beginning to see the difference between RUNG 4 and the other rungs?

In the Living Room/ Family Room

❧

In the games you have been playing with your child, you have helped him or her think about feelings, solutions, and consequences to problems that occur. The focus in the living room/family room is on Consequences, and these exercises will help your children further practice these skills. Problem solvers who think about the consequences of their actions respond to daily conflicts in reasonable and responsible ways because they learn to evaluate the impact of their solutions on themselves and others before they act.

In the Parent's Pages, you have been practicing the first three parts of RUNG 4 of the ICPS Dialogue Ladder. You will now focus upon all four parts of the ICPS dialogue process: (1) ICPS words, (2) Feelings, (3) Alternatives/Solutions, and (4) Consequences. You will now be completely on RUNG 4.

First, a review of ICPS words. Decide how much of the reviews your child may need.

ICPS WORD PAIRS: SET I

IS/IS NOT   AND/OR   SAME/DIFFERENT
SOME/ALL   BEFORE/AFTER   NOW/LATER

Materials Needed

Crayons (any colors)

Directions

Use figure 12.

Fig. 12

Parent Script

Color the picture that IS the TV set.

Circle a picture that is NOT a table.

Point to the couch but NOT the TV.

Color the couch AND the floor but NOT the chair.

Point to SOME of the windows, NOT ALL of them.

How are the table *(point)* AND the couch *(point)* the SAME? (e.g., they both have legs)

How are the table AND the couch DIFFERENT?

Color the curtains on SOME, NOT ALL, of the windows.

Did you color the curtains BEFORE OR AFTER you colored the couch?

Color ALL of the curtains NOW.

OUR LIVING ROOM/FAMILY ROOM

Directions

Ask the questions below in your actual living or family room.

Parent Script

Show me something in this room that IS brown.

Are ALL the (tables) in this room brown?

Is that (table) brown SOME OF THE TIME or ALL OF THE TIME?

Show me something that is a DIFFERENT color.

Show me something that IS round.

Show me something that is NOT round.

Show me a couch AND a chair AND a rug, but NOT a table. *(Add more things to show, as many as child can remember, e.g., couch AND chair AND rug AND . . .)*

This table is NOT a giraffe. What else is it NOT?

(If child names another animal, ask): What is *it NOT that is DIFFERENT from an animal?*

ICPS WORD PAIRS: SET 2

SOME OF THE TIME/ALL OF THE TIME
AT THE SAME TIME/NOT THE SAME TIME

Parent Script

Can you sit on the floor AND watch TV AT THE SAME TIME?

What else can you do AT THE SAME TIME?

Can you sit on the couch AND sit on the floor AT THE SAME TIME?

What else can you NOT do in the living room AT THE SAME TIME?

Are you in the living room ALL OF THE TIME or SOME OF THE TIME?

WHILE WATCHING TV

We are watching (*Sesame Street*). We are NOT watching (*let child answer*).

Are we watching (*Sesame Street*) OR (*name show you are watching*).

I like (*name a TV show*). What TV show do you like?

Do we like the SAME TV show or DIFFERENT ones?

Did we eat dinner BEFORE or AFTER we turned on the TV?

What else did you do BEFORE we turned on the TV?

Do we watch TV SOME OF THE TIME or ALL OF THE TIME?

MY CHILD'S IDEAS WORKSHEET

DATE _____

Directions: Date this page as a way to log your child's progress.

IS/IS NOT

    _____
    _____

AND/OR

    _____
    _____

SAME/DIFFERENT

    _____
    _____

SOME/ALL

    _____
    _____

BEFORE/AFTER

    _____
    _____

NOW/LATER

    _____
    _____

ALL OF THE TIME/
SOME OF THE TIME

    _____
    _____

TWO THINGS AT THE
SAME TIME

    _____
    _____

ICPS WORD PAIRS: SET 3

MIGHT/MAYBE   WHY/BECAUSE
GOOD TIME/NOT A GOOD TIME   GOOD PLACE/NOT A GOOD PLACE
GOOD IDEA/NOT A GOOD IDEA

Directions

Point to the pictures below and ask the following questions. Your child can point to the feeling faces.

Parent Script

Child Is Running Inside

(Point to figure 13a.) What is happening in this picture?

Is this a GOOD IDEA or NOT A GOOD IDEA?

What MIGHT happen if this boy runs inside?

(If "he'll get yelled at" or another nonempathetic consequence is given, ask): "What else MIGHT happen?"

How MIGHT his mom (dad) feel if he falls (gets hurt, bumps into the furniture, knocks something over)?

Fig. 13a

How MIGHT *he* feel if that happens?

Can you think of a DIFFERENT way that this boy can get around this room so that will NOT happen?

Child Is Sitting on the Couch with Her Shoes On

(Point to figure 13b.)

What is happening in this picture?

Is this a GOOD PLACE for her shoes?

What MIGHT happen if she puts her shoes on the couch?

How will her mom (dad) feel if she does that?

Where IS a good place for her shoes?

Do you see anything else in this picture that is NOT A GOOD IDEA?

(If needed): Is the couch a GOOD PLACE to drink (juice)?

WHY (WHY NOT)?

Where is a GOOD PLACE to drink (juice)?

Fig. 13b

SEQUENCING

Purpose

To review focusing on the timing of events, what happens *before* and what happens *after* one carries out an act, and whether an idea (place, time) is a good one. These are all skills that will later help children think of consequences to behavior.

Directions

Use figure 14. (The frames are not in the correct order.) Option: Duplicate this page, cut figure 14 into separate pictures, and ask your child to place them in order as you ask each question.

Parent Script

What happens first? Point to the picture that shows what happens first.

Then what?

Did the girl turn on the TV BEFORE or AFTER she walked over to it?

Then what happens?

Did she sit down to watch the TV BEFORE or AFTER she turned it on?

What MIGHT have happened BEFORE she walked over to turn on the TV? Just make it up.

What MIGHT happen AFTER the girl sits down to watch TV? Just make it up.

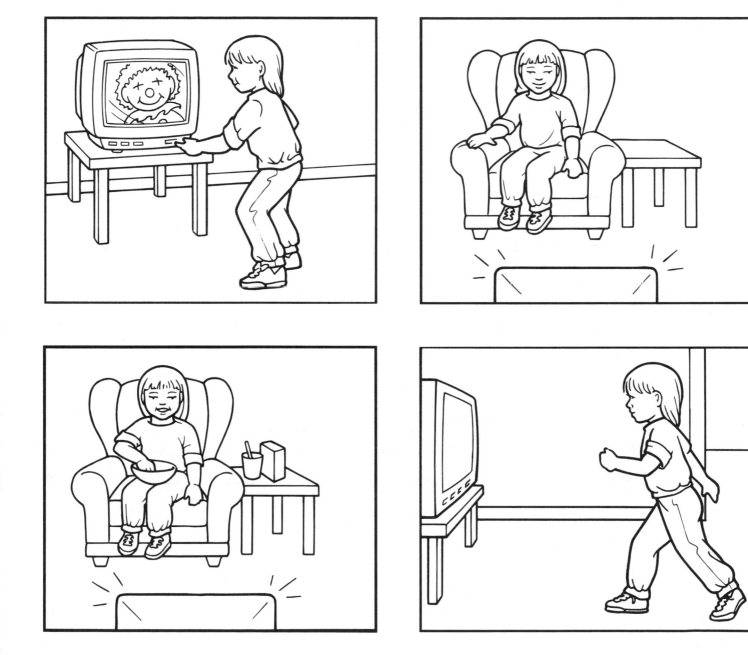

Fig. 14

PARENT AND CHILD EXCHANGE

Write what you do or say when your child is having a problem with you or another adult. That is, write what you and your child typically do or say.

Sample Problems (Potential Harm)

1. Your child leaves toys in the middle of the floor.
2. Your child is jumping on a chair.

If neither problem has ever occurred, just make up what you and your child might do or say.

Problem

_____

I did (said): _____

_____

Child: _____

Parent: _____

_____

Child: _____

Parent: _____

_____

Child: _____

Parent: _____

_____

Child: _____

Is this exchange a monologue or a dialogue? Determine which rung of the ICPS Dialogue Ladder you are on now by comparing your statements or questions with those on the next page. On each rung of the ladder, check off those statements that best match your own, and write any other statements in the blank lines of the rung that best fits the *style* of your statements.

THE ICPS DIALOGUE LADDER

ICPS Dialoguing: The Problem-Solving Process

_____ Is that a GOOD PLACE to jump (leave your toys)?

_____ What MIGHT happen if you do that?

_____ How MIGHT I (you) feel if that happens?

_____ What can you do so that will NOT happen?

_____ _____

Suggestions with Explanation, Including Feelings

_____ You might fall and hurt yourself (someone might trip over your toys).

_____ I (you) will feel very sad if you (someone) get(s) hurt.

_____ I get angry when you do that (don't do what I ask).

_____ Where is a DIFFERENT place to put your toys?

_____ _____

Suggestions Without Explanation

_____ Jump on the floor (toys go in your room).

_____ Chairs are for sitting, not jumping.

_____ _____

Commands, Demands, Belittles, Punishes

_____ Don't leave your toys (jump) there!

_____ You made a mess! Go to your room!

_____ Do you want a spanking (etc.)?

_____ _____

RUNG 4

RUNG 3

RUNG 2

RUNG 1

Have you climbed to the top, to RUNG 4, using all four parts of that rung?

1. ICPS Words
2. Feelings
3. Solutions
4. Consequences

This is what we call Full ICPS Dialoguing. If you are on RUNG 4, you are now freeing your child to think.

Note: Some children will respond to this new way of talking more quickly than others. Although asking rather than telling may take more time in the beginning, you should eventually see the positive behaviors you want, and in the end it will take less time than with the methods of discipline you may have used in the past.

DISSECTING THE ICPS DIALOGUE LADDER

Focus: ICPS Words, Feelings, Solutions, and Consequences

Consequences are the direct actions by one person (B) as a result of an action by another person (A). For example, if A hits B, B might hit A back. Therefore, children are guided to think of consequences with the question "What MIGHT happen next if . . . ?"

You can now practice using all four parts of RUNG 4 dialoguing that your child enjoyed in the games. In the blank lines provided below, fill in ways to use each part of the ladder.

Problem

Your child is watching TV when she should be doing homework.

ICPS Words (Samples)

Is this a GOOD TIME or NOT A GOOD TIME to watch TV?

WHY is this a *(repeat child's answer)*?

(Add your own ideas for question with ICPS Words.)

_____

_____

_____

Add Feelings

How MIGHT I feel when you keep putting off your homework?

Do you and I feel the SAME way OR DIFFERENT ways about this?

(Add your own ideas for questions using Feeling Words.)

_____

_____

_____

Add Solutions

If you do NOT want to do your homework NOW, can you think of another GOOD TIME so you will get it done BEFORE you go to bed?

(Add your own ideas on how to help your child solve this problem.)

_____

_____

_____

Add Consequences

OK. You made this decision. IF you do NOT get your homework done by bedtime, what MIGHT happen next?

How MIGHT you feel if that happens?

Try your plan and we'll see how that works out.

(Add your own ideas for how to help your child decide whether his or her solution IS or IS NOT a good one, in light of potential consequences and including feelings.)

_____

_____

_____

On RUNG 4, not all problems lead to ICPS dialogue that follows the same order: Words, Feelings, Solutions, Consequences. In the example below, "Child is playing too near a fragile flower pot," the first part retains the use of ICPS Words. The next logical question skips to potential Consequences of this behavior, with thinking about Feelings relevant to the consequence (e.g., the pot might break), not the original behavior (playing too close to it).

Problem

Child is playing too near a fragile flower pot. Here's how the entire dialogue might go:

Is near the flower pot a GOOD PLACE OR NOT A GOOD PLACE for you to play? *(word pair)*

What MIGHT happen if you play here? *(consequence)*

How MIGHT I feel if that happens? *(parent's feelings)*

How MIGHT *you* feel if that happens? *(child's feelings)*

Do you think we'll feel the SAME way OR DIFFERENT ways?

Can you think of a DIFFERENT place to play so that will NOT happen? *(solution)*

Shortening the Dialogue

You will soon develop a feel for which questions are needed and in which order. In time, you won't need to use all four parts of the dialogue on RUNG 4. Once you and your children are familiar and comfortable with this kind of exchange, all you need to ask may be:

Is this A GOOD IDEA (GOOD TIME; GOOD PLACE) for _____?

What's a DIFFERENT way (TIME; PLACE) to do that?

Can you think of a DIFFERENT way to tell me how you feel?

Your child is standing in front of the TV screen, blocking your view.
How could you shorten a RUNG 4 dialogue by not using all four parts of the rung?

_____

_____

_____

Would you still use any statements below RUNG 4 if your child actually stood in front of the TV while you were trying to watch it? If so, check off those that most closely match what you would say, and write in any not shown on the blank line of the rung that best fits the *style* of your statements.

THE ICPS DIALOGUE LADDER

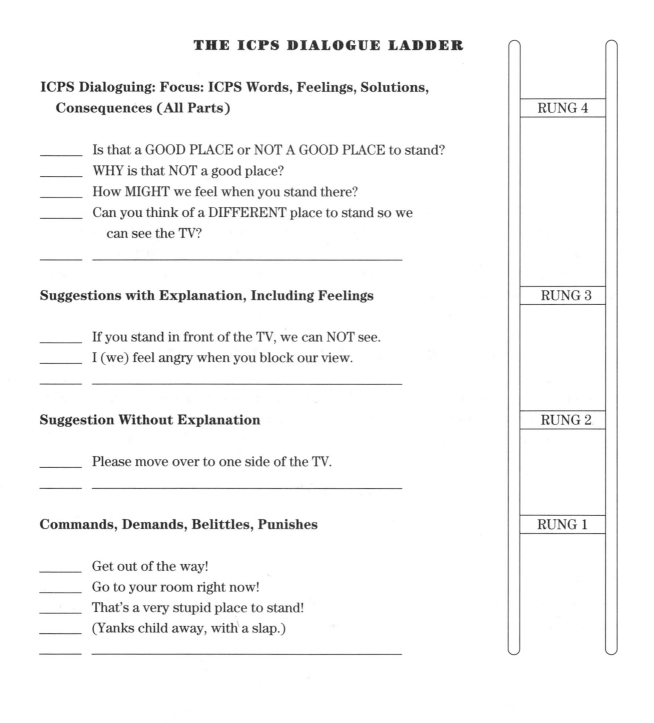

ICPS Dialoguing: Focus: ICPS Words, Feelings, Solutions, Consequences (All Parts)

RUNG 4

_____ Is that a GOOD PLACE or NOT A GOOD PLACE to stand?
_____ WHY is that NOT a good place?
_____ How MIGHT we feel when you stand there?
_____ Can you think of a DIFFERENT place to stand so we
     can see the TV?

_____ _____

Suggestions with Explanation, Including Feelings

RUNG 3

_____ If you stand in front of the TV, we can NOT see.
_____ I (we) feel angry when you block our view.

_____ _____

Suggestion Without Explanation

RUNG 2

_____ Please move over to one side of the TV.

_____ _____

Commands, Demands, Belittles, Punishes

RUNG 1

_____ Get out of the way!
_____ Go to your room right now!
_____ That's a very stupid place to stand!
_____ (Yanks child away, with a slap.)

_____ _____

Further Exercises

❧

The previous sections of this workbook were designed to help you practice specific ways to help your children learn how to think and solve everyday problems. While previous problems were room specific, many problem situations and things people have feelings about do not take place in any specific room in the house. Below are some further exercises for you and your child to enhance your understanding of each other.

HOW DO YOU FEEL ABOUT THAT?

To further mutual sensitivity to each other's feelings and preferences, the first exercise will help you and your child learn more about how those feelings and preferences are the same and how they are different.

Parent Script

I'm going to write down things that I do or say that I think make *you* feel HAPPY. Don't tell me. I'm going to guess.

(Write your thoughts in the left-hand column on the next page.)

Now you tell me what you think I do or say that makes *you* feel HAPPY. *(Write child's responses in right-hand column on the next page.)*

YOUR IDEAS OF WHAT YOU DO OR SAY TO MAKE CHILD HAPPY	CHILD'S IDEAS OF WHAT YOU DO OR SAY TO MAKE HIM OR HER HAPPY
_____	_____
_____	_____
_____	_____
_____	_____
_____	_____

(Compare how many responses are the same and how many are different. Circle those that are DIFFERENT. Begin questions with those that are DIFFERENT.)

Parent Script

I thought _____ makes you feel HAPPY.

You did not tell me about that.

How do you feel about that?

WHY does that make you feel that way?

(Repeat the above question for each idea you listed that your child did not. Now turn to those that are the same.)

You said that when I _____ , that makes you HAPPY, and I said that too.

Did we say the SAME thing? *(Let child answer)*. Yes, we said the SAME thing.

(Repeat for all the SAME things.)

HOW DO I FEEL ABOUT THAT?

Parent Script

Now we're going to change the game. First, I'm going to write down some things that I think you would say that you do or say that *I* feel HAPPY about. Don't tell me. I'm going to guess. *(Write your thoughts in the left-hand column on the next page.)*

Now tell me some things *you* think you do or say that I feel HAPPY about. I'm going to write them down here. *(Write in the right-hand column on the next page.)*

WHAT YOU THINK CHILD WOULD SAY HE/SHE DOES TO MAKE YOU HAPPY	CHILD SAYS WHAT HE/SHE DOES TO MAKE YOU HAPPY
_____	_____
_____	_____
_____	_____
_____	_____
_____	_____

(Compare how many are the same and how many are different. Circle those that are different. Begin with those that are DIFFERENT.)

Parent Script

You thought _____ makes me feel happy.

I did NOT think of that.

Yes, it does (no, it does NOT) make me feel HAPPY.

Can you tell me WHY that does (does NOT) make me feel HAPPY?

(Repeat the above questions for each idea the child listed but you did not. Tell your child if his or her idea does or does not make you feel happy, and ask your child to try to tell you why.)

(Now turn to those that are the SAME.)

You said _____ makes me feel happy, and I did too.

Did we say the SAME thing? *(Child answers).* Yes, we said the SAME thing.

(Option): I'm going to read what I think you do that makes me feel HAPPY, and then I'm going to read what you said you do that makes me feel that way. Listen carefully. Tell me which ones are the SAME.

DO WE FEEL THE SAME WAY ABOUT THAT?

The following exercise was designed to help your children better appreciate that DIFFERENT people can feel DIFFERENT ways about the SAME thing.

Parent Script

What do you like to get for your birthday?

Do you think I would like the SAME thing OR something DIFFERENT?

Think of something that you would like to have that I might NOT like to have.

What might I like to have that you would NOT like to have?

WHAT'S HAPPENING HERE?

On the next page is one example of a problem situation between a parent and a child that can occur in more than one room in the house.

Purpose

This game has two purposes: (1) to help your child cope with the frustration of not being able to talk with you when you are busy, and (2) to review for you a short, simple RUNG 4 dialogue.

Directions

Use figure 15.

Problem

Child interrupts Mom on the phone.

Parent Script

Can this mom talk to her friend and to her child AT THE SAME TIME?

How might her friend feel if she talks to her child now?

This mom can talk to her child LATER.

What can this girl do while she waits? *(Record child's response).*

_____

Anything else? _____

Fig. 15

In the previous exercise, this mom asked her child "What can you do while you wait?" Had she said, "Why don't you go watch TV?" would the child have done that? Think of any problem situation that actually comes up between you and your children. It can be a problem not already covered in a specific room, such as

1. spilling food on the kitchen floor, or
2. touching a hot saucer on the stove.

It can be a problem that is not room specific or even house specific, such as

1. refusing to come in from playing outside at bedtime,
2. wanting you to buy candy in the grocery store, or
3. demanding attention in the car while you're driving.

Remember, these problems are NOT between two or more children. They are the kind of problems that come up between you and your child.

PARENT AND CHILD EXCHANGE

Directions

Record an actual problem that came up between you and your child. Next record the actual exchange that occurred. As always, you do not have to use the same number of lines provided.

Problem

_____

I did (said): _____

_____

Child: _____

Parent: _____

_____

Child: _____

Parent: _____

_____

Child: _____

Parent: _____

_____

Child: _____

If needed, write what you might ask to make for a better RUNG 4 fit. Use a shortened version. Name the part of the rung you would use: ICPS Words, Feelings, Solutions, Consequences.

_____

_____

_____

On the following pages record real problems that come up, and the actual exchanges between you and your child, on the lines provided.

For any problems already covered on an ICPS Dialogue Ladder, you can look back and see which rung you are on now. You may also notice a change in how your child responds as well.

Problem

_____

I did (said): _____

_____

Child: _____

Parent: _____

_____

Child: _____

Parent: _____

_____

Child: _____

Parent: _____

_____

Child: _____

Problem

_____

I did (said): _____

_____

Child: _____

Parent: _____

_____

Child: _____

Parent: _____

_____

Child: _____

Parent: _____

_____

Child: _____

Problem

_____

I did (said): _____

_____

Child: _____

Parent: _____

_____

Child: _____

Parent: _____

_____

Child: _____

Parent: _____

_____

Child: _____

Problem

_____

I did (said): _____

_____

Child: _____

Parent: _____

_____

Child: _____

Parent: _____

_____

Child: _____

Parent: _____

_____

Child: _____

Use extra paper for any additional problems you wish to record.

Keep these pages for easy access. If you get stuck along the way, refer to the Parent/Child Problem ICPS Dialogue Reminders in the back of this book. See where you need more practice. For example, did you ask your child about his or her feelings and your own?

Now fill in Log A2 on the next page and compare your approach and your child's behavior to Log A1 on page 10 that you completed before you began to use this workbook.

LOG A₂

I Can Problem Solve (ICPS): Parent and Child Exchanges

Date	Problem Situation	Parent Actions/ Statements/Questions	Child's Responses	Conclusion	Outcome (Positive + Neutral 0 Negative –)
6/5/95	Lori still interrupts occasionally.	Can I talk to you and to my friend at the same time?	No, and I can think of something different to do.	Lori gets a puzzle off her shelf.	+ We both felt happy and proud.

REAL-LIFE ANECDOTES: PARENT/CHILD PROBLEMS

In addition to the behaviors you just charted, you may want to log some other interesting changes in your children from the time you began this workbook until now.

Do your children use the ICPS Words *NOT*, *SAME*, *DIFFERENT*, *BEFORE*, *AFTER*, and so on, more, less, or about the same now as before you began this workbook? _____

WORD   **HOW USED**

_____   _____

_____   _____

_____   _____

Do your children tell you how they feel and use the words *HAPPY*, *SAD*, etc. more, less, or about the same as before? _____

FEELING WORD   **HOW USED**
                                          (ABOUT THEIR FEELINGS)

_____   _____

_____   _____

_____   _____

Do your children use the words *HAPPY*, *SAD*, etc. in reference to how *you* feel more, less, or about the same? _____

FEELING WORD   **HOW USED**
                                          (ABOUT YOUR FEELINGS)

_____   _____

_____   _____

_____   _____

When your children cannot have something they want from you (such as candy), or when you are otherwise angry or displeased, do they react any differently than before you began ICPS?

Before ICPS

_____

_____

_____

After ICPS

_____

_____

_____

Are there any other anecdotes relating to parent/child situations, either positive, non-problem situations or conflict, or other problem situations that show interesting changes in your children?

Before ICPS

_____

_____

_____

After ICPS

_____

_____

_____

Part 2

❦

Child/Child Situations

In Part 1 you practiced ways of dialoguing that helped you move up the rungs of the ICPS Dialogue Ladder. Now it is your child's turn. You have been teaching your child ICPS Words and how to think about Feelings, Solutions, and Consequences, which means he or she is ready for this next very important step in becoming a thinking child.

Your goal in Part 2 is to have your child reach the top level of thinking skills, be a good problem solver, and not show aggressive or withdrawn behaviors when things don't go right.

On the next page is Log B_1, illustrating common behaviors children display when they are frustrated or angry. Before you continue with the rest of this workbook, take a minute to use this worksheet to identify how your child usually behaves.

Check the line under the description that most accurately identifies how your child responds to frustration, disappointment, and conflict. Again, if you have more than one child, duplicate this page and observe each one separately.

This same log appears again as B_2 at the end of Part 2 to help you track your children's progress.

DATE _____

> **A Problem Solver**
> Able to negotiate
> to reach a goal,
> or able to wait for
> what she or he wants

———

*Becoming a
Problem Solver*
Tries *more* than one
solution. But, if fails,
still retreats, gives up.

———

*Becoming a
Problem Solver*
Tries *more* than one
solution. But, if fails,
resorts to emotion.

———

*Early Attempt to
Problem Solve*
Tries one solution.
If fails, walks away.

*Early Attempt to
Problem Solve*
Tries one solution.
If fails, gets upset.

———

*Nonthinking, Emotional
Responses*
crying
sullen
hovering
hiding

———

*Nonthinking, Emotional
Responses*
arguing
fighting
hitting
curse words

———

Shy/Withdrawn

Aggressive

Kids Might Like Different Things Too

❧

Purpose

To help children recognize how their own feelings and preferences may be the same or different from those of other children, an important skill for later problem solving.

Materials

Crayons (yellow, blue, red, purple, orange, green)

Directions

This game is to be played with two or more children, one child at a time. *Have one child use figure 16a and another 16b. You may wish to duplicate 16a and 16b before the children color them or tear them out later in the game. If more than two children are playing, duplicate additional copies.*

Parent Script

(To first child): Color ALL the things that make you feel HAPPY yellow. If nothing you see makes you happy, say the word *nothing*.

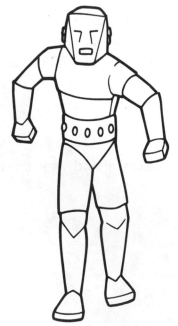

Fig. 16a

(When finished): Now, color ALL the things that make you feel SAD blue. If nothing makes you sad, say the word *nothing.*

(When finished): Now, color ALL the things that make you feel ANGRY red. If nothing makes you angry, say the word *nothing.*

(When finished): Color ALL the things that make you feel AFRAID purple. If nothing, say the word *nothing.*

(When finished): Color ALL the things that make you feel PROUD orange. If nothing, say the word *nothing.*

(When finished): Color ALL the things that make you feel FRUSTRATED green. If nothing, say the word *nothing.*

Have the second child color 16b when the child who went first is not around.

Parent Script

(To second child): Color ALL the things that make you feel HAPPY yellow. If nothing you see makes you happy, say the word *nothing.*

(When finished): Now, color ALL the things that make you feel SAD blue. If nothing makes you sad, say the word *nothing.*

(When finished): Now, color ALL the things that make you feel ANGRY red. If nothing makes you angry, say the word *nothing.*

(When finished): Color ALL the things that make you feel AFRAID purple. If nothing, say the word *nothing.*

(When finished): Color ALL the things that make you feel PROUD orange. If nothing, say the word *nothing.*

(When finished): Color ALL the things that make you feel FRUSTRATED green. If nothing, say the word *nothing.*

Directions

Before bringing the two (or more) children together to discuss the pictures, ask the first child the following questions. Record that child's answers on the lines provided.

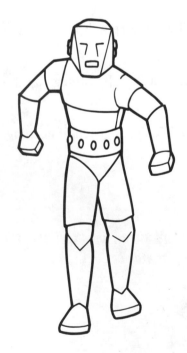

Fig. 16b

Parent Script

How do you think your sister (brother, cousin, friend) MIGHT feel about this? *(Point to each picture as you ask the questions below.)*

The dog?_____

The broken doll? _____

Swimming? _____

The doll? _____

The robot? _____

The broken window? _____

Melted ice cream? _____

The overturned truck? _____

Now tear out pictures 16a and 16b (or use the duplicated pictures the children colored) and put them side by side. Bring in the child who colored second (and any others who participated) and ask the following questions.

Parent Script

(To one child): Remember, you colored the things you feel HAPPY about YELLOW. Point to ALL the pictures that you both (all) colored YELLOW. Do you feel the SAME way or a DIFFERENT way about this (these)?

(To another child): Point to a picture that you colored YELLOW that your brother (sister, friend, cousin) did NOT color YELLOW. Do you feel the SAME way or a DIFFERENT way about this?

(To child who did not color picture yellow): How do you feel about this?

(To first child): WHY do you feel HAPPY about this?

(To second child): WHY do you feel *(repeat answer)* about this?

Repeat, taking turns among the children, with all differences with the word HAPPY. Repeat above questions with each feeling word.

Do They Feel the Same Way About This?

❧

Purpose

To further appreciate that two children can feel different ways about the same thing.

Directions

Use Figure 17.

Fig. 17

Parent Script

What's happening in this picture?

Do this boy *(point)* and this boy *(point)* feel the SAME way OR DIFFERENT ways about this TV show?

How does this boy *(point)* feel?

How does that boy *(point)* feel?

WHY MIGHT that boy *(point to the afraid boy)* feel the way he does about the TV show?

Any other reason? Another BECAUSE?

WHY MIGHT this boy *(point to happy boy)* feel the way he does?

Any other reason?

Is it OK for DIFFERENT people to feel DIFFERENT ways about the SAME thing?

Yes, it IS OK.

DIFFERENT CHOICES

Below is a typical problem, and one way a parent can handle it. For each statement or question from the parent, write in which rung of the ICPS ladder you think it falls on.

RUNG 1: *Commands, Demands, Belittles, Punishes*
RUNG 2: *Suggestions Without Explanation*
RUNG 3: *Suggestions with Explanation, Including Feelings*
RUNG 4: *ICPS Dialoguing: The Problem-Solving Process*

"He won't play with me."

Child: Mommy, Mark won't play with me.
Mom: Why don't you play with someone else, Cindy?   RUNG _____
Child: I want to play with Mark.
Mom: Why don't you play with your new spinning top?   RUNG _____
Child: I don't want to!
Mom: Cindy, you can't always expect people to do what you want. RUNG _____

Answer ("He won't play with me.")

Mom: Why don't you play with someone else, Cindy?   RUNG __2__
Mom: Why don't you play with your new spinning top?   RUNG __2__
Mom: Cindy, you can't always expect people to do what you want. RUNG __3__

The last statement could also be RUNG 1 if tone of voice reflects exasperation or sounds like a put-down. Any further talk is essentially cut off.

Sample ICPS RUNG 4 Dialogue

The dialogue below shows how Cindy's mother helped Cindy understand whether or not she was really being rejected, or whether or not the *activity* she suggested, jumping rope, was really what was being rejected.

Mom: What do you want to do, Cindy?
Cindy: Jump rope.
Mom: Do you want to jump rope or play with Mark?
Cindy: Play with Mark.

Mom: Do you think Mark and you feel the SAME way or DIFFERENT ways about jumping rope?

Cindy: Different ways?

Mom: Can you think of something to do so Mark will want to play with you? Something he would like to do too?

If Mark actually did not want to play with Cindy at that time, what questions could you ask her to help her cope with the frustration?

Hint: Use the words DIFFERENT, NOW, and AT THE SAME TIME.

_____

_____

_____

Answer

Mom: What is Mark doing NOW?

Mom: Can he do that AND play with you AT THE SAME TIME?

Mom: Can you think of something DIFFERENT to do NOW while you wait?

Is That a Good Idea?

❧

Purpose

To begin to think about the potential impact of acts on the feelings of other children.

Materials

Crayon (any color) or pencil

Directions

Use figures 18a–c. Point to each picture as you ask the corresponding questions.

Parent Script

Two Boys Are Sharing a Truck

(Point to picture 18a.)

What is happening in this picture?

If you think what is happening IS A GOOD IDEA, draw a HAPPY face here. *(Point to circle under picture.)*

If you think this is NOT A GOOD IDEA, draw a SAD face.

Hint: If you do not agree with your child's choice, do not correct him or her. Your child will evaluate these acts of behavior as part of this activity. By letting your child express his or her feelings, you may learn something important about what's on your child's mind.

WHY do you think that IS (IS NOT) a good idea?

How MIGHT one boy *(point)* who IS sharing feel?

How MIGHT the other boy *(point)* feel?

WHY do you think they MIGHT feel that way?

(If not a good idea): What can they do that IS a GOOD IDEA?

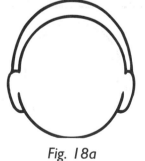

Fig. 18a

Girl Making Face

(Point to figure 18b.)

What is happening in this picture?

If you think what is happening IS A GOOD IDEA, draw a HAPPY face here. *(Point to circle under picture.)*

If you think this is NOT A GOOD IDEA, draw a SAD face.

WHY do you think that IS (IS NOT) a GOOD IDEA?

How MIGHT the other girl feel?

(If not a good idea): What can the girl who is teasing do that IS A GOOD IDEA?

(If child believes teasing is a good idea, ask why. Then ask, "What might happen if [repeat child's answer]." You might then ask): "What can she do that IS a GOOD IDEA so she will NOT feel that way (so that will NOT happen)?*

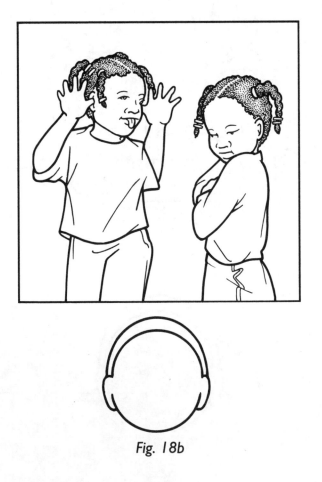

Fig. 18b

Boy Helping Boy Who Fell Get Up

(Point to figure 18c.)

What is happening in this picture?

If you think what is happening IS A GOOD IDEA, draw a HAPPY face here. *(Point to circle under picture.)*

If you think this is NOT A GOOD IDEA, draw a SAD face.

WHY do you think that IS (IS NOT) a GOOD IDEA?

(If not a good idea, ask why. Then ask): What can the boy do that IS A GOOD IDEA?

How MIGHT the boy who is being helped feel?

How MIGHT the boy who is helping feel?

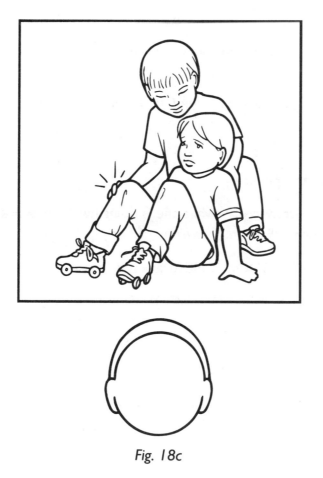

Fig. 18c

Is That a Good Time?

❦

Purpose

To think about timing as an important part of problem solving with other children.

Boy Interrupting Girl Doing Homework

(Point to figure 19.)

What is happening in this picture?

If you think asking his sister to play while she is doing her homework IS A GOOD TIME, draw a HAPPY face here. *(Point to circle under picture.)*

If you think this is NOT A GOOD TIME, draw a SAD face.

WHY do you think that IS (IS NOT) A GOOD TIME?

How MIGHT his sister feel?

WHY do you think she feels that way?

When IS A GOOD TIME to ask his sister to play?

What can he do while he waits that IS A GOOD IDEA and so she will NOT feel that way?

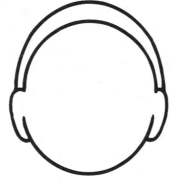

Fig. 19

PARENT AND CHILD EXCHANGE

Record what you do, or what you might do, should the following arise.

Problem

Child interrupts another child.

Parent: _____

_____

Child: _____

Parent: _____

_____

Child: _____

Now predict which rung or rungs of the ICPS Dialogue Ladder this exchange most closely resembles, and check off on the next page where the responses actually fall. If you didn't use the following ICPS words in your exchange, add some new questions that include them in the lines provided below.

A Good Time/Not a Good Time?

_____   _____

At the Same Time?

_____   _____

Now/Later?

_____   _____

Fill in the number of the rung that best fits the *style* of your questions. Is your exchange the same or different than it was before beginning this workbook?

THE ICPS DIALOGUE LADDER

ICPS Dialoguing: The Problem-Solving Process

_____ Can (your brother) play with you and (do his homework)
AT THE SAME TIME?

_____ Is asking your brother to play when he is busy
A GOOD TIME or NOT A GOOD TIME?

_____ WHY do you think that?

_____ How MIGHT your brother feel if you do that?

_____ What MIGHT happen next?

_____ How MIGHT you (he) feel if that happens?

_____ What can you do while you wait (NOW) that
IS A GOOD IDEA?

_____ _____

Suggestions with Explanation, Including Feelings

_____ Your (brother) feels angry when you _____.

_____ He won't play with you if you bother him.

_____ _____

Suggestions Without Explanation

_____ Why don't you read while you wait?

_____ _____

Commands, Demands, Belittles, Punishes

_____ Don't bother (your brother)!

_____ Go to your room! You're bothering him.

_____ _____

RUNG 4

RUNG 3

RUNG 2

RUNG 1

Let's Make Up a Story: The Bike

❧

Purpose

To foster sensitivity to other people's feelings, and to enhance listening skills by remembering what is in a story.

Materials

Crayons (any colors) and/or a pencil (for faces)

Directions

Use figures 20a–b.

First, read the story, and let your child fill in the blanks verbally. Second, on the lines provided write the story your child creates. Third, reread the story and let your child draw in the squares. Fourth, ask your child to retell the part of the story he or she created. Fifth, your child can draw anything he or she desires about what happened in the story.

Parent Script

I'm going to tell you a story. It's called "The Bike." You're going to help me make up part of this story, and I'm going to write down what you say. You have to remember the whole story. Are you ready?

Fig. 20a

Richard and Dawn were riding a bike together. They felt very _____. *(If child says "I don't know," say):* You can just make it up. *(If needed, ask):* HAPPY or SAD? OK, draw a *(repeat feeling word child gave you)* face for each of these children *(point to blank faces on drawing).*

Did they feel the SAME way OR DIFFERENT ways?

Well, Dawn's bike was very old.

When Dawn started to ride it again, the wheels came flying off.

Dawn started to cry.

Now she felt very _____ .

Richard was her friend.

When the wheels of Dawn's bike came flying off, he felt _____ .

Tracey loved to tease Dawn.

When Tracey saw the wheel come off, she laughed.

Tracey said, "I'm glad your old wheel came off. Ha, ha, ha."

Fig. 20b

Now Dawn felt _____ .

Richard did NOT like the way Tracey was teasing his friend.

Richard felt _____ .

What happens next in this story? You make it up. I'll write what you tell me here.

_____

_____

_____

_____

_____

_____

_____

_____

_____

_____

Directions

Let your child color the pictures now. Then reread the story as below. Write your child's answers on the blank lines and let them draw faces in the squares.

Richard and Dawn were riding their bikes together. They felt very _____ .

Draw how they felt in this square.

Well, Dawn's bike was very old.

When Dawn started to ride it again, what happened to the wheels? _____ .

Yes, the wheels came flying off.

Dawn started to cry.
Now she felt very _____ .

Tracey loved to tease Dawn.

When Tracey saw the wheels come off, she thought that was very funny. Ha, ha, ha.

Now Dawn felt _____ .

And Richard felt _____ .

Do you remember the rest of the story you made up?
Tell me what you said happened next.

_____

_____

_____

_____

_____

_____

_____

_____

_____

You can draw something that happens in this story here.

My Own Story

❧

Purpose

To strengthen willingness and ability to express one's own feelings in a problem situation. Children who recognize and are sensitive to their own feelings will more likely recognize and be sensitive to how other people feel.

Materials

Crayons (any color) or pencil

Directions

First, ask your child to draw a picture. Second, he or she creates a story for you to write down. Third, your child draws a new picture. Fourth, he or she creates a new story and you write that down too.

Parent Script

Today we're going to do something DIFFERENT with ICPS.

Do you remember what ICPS means? *(if needed):* I Can Problem Solve.

I want you to draw something that you did today, something that happened to you, or anything that made you feel HAPPY OR SAD OR ANGRY (MAD) OR SCARED (AFRAID).

If you draw something that made you feel a DIFFERENT way than those I just said, that's OK. Just tell me the feeling that you are drawing about.

Tell me about your drawing.

_____

_____

_____

_____

_____

_____

Now draw something that made you feel a DIFFERENT way from what you just drew. It can be something that made you feel HAPPY or SAD or ANGRY or AFRAID. Or maybe PROUD or FRUSTRATED. Tell me about this drawing.

Note: You may wish to encourage your child to use a separate sketch book or loose paper and draw about other real or make-believe situations.

What's the Problem?

❧

Purpose

To recognize the need to think about what the problem really is before it can be solved.

Materials

Crayons to color picture, or a pencil to draw in faces

Directions

Use figure 21. If more than one child is doing this exercise, ask each child to pick someone who has a problem, and draw in the face.

Parent Script

Who has the problem here?

Draw a SAD or an ANGRY face on the child you think has the problem.

(If one child, say): I see a problem too. *(Draw a face.)* Do you and I see the SAME problem OR DIFFERENT problems? Tell me about the problem the child you picked might be having.

(If more than one child, ask): Do you see the SAME problem as *(name another child)* or a DIFFERENT problem?

Sometimes we think we know what the problem is just by looking, you know, by seeing with our _____ *(point to your eyes)*. If these were real people, how else could we find out?

(If needed): Could we tell them OR could we ASK them?

Fig. 21

FINDING THE REAL PROBLEM

As you read the parent and child exchange below, decide which rung of the ICPS ladder each of Mom's questions or statements are on.

RUNG 1: Commands, Demands, Belittles, Punishes
RUNG 2: Suggestions Without Explanation
RUNG 3: Suggestions with Explanation, Including Feelings
RUNG 4: ICPS Dialoguing: The Problem-Solving Process

In my book *Raising a Thinking Child*, a mother talks to her four-year-old son Alex about sharing toys. Before ICPS, his mom handles it this way:

Mom: Alex, your teacher tells me you grabbed toys again.
       Why did you do that?   RUNG _____

Alex: 'Cause it was my turn.

Mom: You should either play together or take turns. Grabbing is not nice. RUNG _____

Alex: But they're mine!

Mom: You must learn to share your toys. You can't bring them to school
       if you're not going to share them.   RUNG _____
       Jonathan was angry and he won't be your friend.   RUNG _____

Alex: But Mom, he wouldn't give them to me.

Mom: You can't go around grabbing things.   RUNG _____
       You wouldn't like it if he did that to you.   RUNG _____
       Tomorrow, tell him you're sorry.   RUNG _____

Answers to Questions

Mom: Alex, your teacher tells me you grabbed toys again.
       Why did you do that?   RUNG ___1___

In this tone of voice, asking why is more accusatory and is not really a genuine question to seek information. This mom was not listening. She was intent on what she wanted to teach her child without hearing his point of view.

Mom: You should either play together or take turns. Grabbing is not nice. RUNG ___2___

Mom: You must learn to share your toys. You can't bring them to school
       if you're not going to share them.   RUNG ___2___
       Jonathan was angry and he won't be your friend.   RUNG ___3___

Mom: You can't go around grabbing things.　　　　　　　　　RUNG ___2___

　　　You wouldn't like it if he did that to you.　　　　　RUNG ___3___

　　　Tomorrow, tell him you're sorry.　　　　　　　　　RUNG ___2___

By using the ICPS word *BEFORE*, let's see what Alex's mom could find out.

Mom: Alex, your teacher tells me you're grabbing toys again.

　　　Tell me what happened BEFORE you grabbed the toys.

Alex: Jonathan had my magnets. He wouldn't give them back.

By associating the question "What happened?" with the ICPS Word *BEFORE*, the child hears a genuine information-seeking question connected to a word *(BEFORE)* learned in a game the child enjoyed. This is less threatening than the rhetorical, if not accusatory, question "Why did you . . ." which the child knows is not really an information-seeking question—and to which many children respond with an "I don't know," or a shrug of their shoulders, or a lie.

Mom: Why did you have to have them back right then?

Alex: 'Cause he had a long turn.

This "why" question is distinguished from the more threatening "Why . . . !" in that it genuinely asks for more specific information and allows the parent to discover how the child sees the problem.

Question

What did Alex's mom learn from her last question that she could not have learned when she kept demanding that he share? Did she learn that Alex

  a) didn't know any other way to get the toy,
  b) knew another way but chose to grab the toy anyway, or
  c) knew another way but believed he already shared his toy and couldn't get it back any other way?

Answer

  c: If Alex believed he did share his toy, would he listen if Mom kept insisting that he share?

Was Alex's grabbing
- a) the problem, or
- b) his solution to the problem?

Answer

b: Having learned this, the nature of the problem now appeared different.

Question

Using the word *DIFFERENT*, can you think of an ICPS dialogue question that Alex's mom could use next?

_____

_____

_____

Answer

One ICPS dialogue question might be, "Grabbing is *one* way to get your toy back. Can you think of a DIFFERENT way to get your toy back?" The problem shifts from "not sharing" to "how to get the toy back." How does this compare with what you wrote?

One more example: A boy says to his mother, "Mommy, Tommy hit me."

Mom 1: Hit him back!
  Child: But I'm afraid.
  Mom: I don't want you to be so timid.

Mom 2: Don't hit him back. Tell the teacher instead.
  Child: But he'll call me a tattletale.
  Mom: If you don't tell the teacher, kids will keep hitting you.

Question

How are the responses of these two moms different? How are they the same?

They are giving different advice but they both are doing the thinking for the child, first with a RUNG 2 suggestion and then with a RUNG 3 explanation. An ICPS parent might ask, "What happened BEFORE Tommy hit you?" Once the problem is defined, ICPS parents can help the child solve it.

I CAN PROBLEM SOLVE: ALTERNATIVE SOLUTIONS

Ability to think of more than one solution is a key skill in problem solving, one that plays a pivotal role in guiding behavior. Having several options to choose from increases children's chances of success and helps them cope with frustration when they cannot have what they want.

In the exercises that follow, your child will see many different, alternative solutions to problems that occur between two or more children. This will help him or her further appreciate that "There's more than one way to solve a problem" and "I don't have to give up too soon."

When working with solutions, it is important to remember a few key points.

Some Definitions of Terms and Techniques

Solution

Definition: A solution is a way to obtain a goal, such as "Ask him," "Take turns," "Tell Mom he won't let me play," or "Hit him."

Technique: Do not place value judgments on solutions at this time. Your child will decide whether or not his or her own idea IS or IS NOT a good one in the next section, that of consequential thinking. After one solution is given, say, "That's *one* way. The idea of this game is to think of lots of DIFFERENT ways. Can you think of way number two?"

Enumeration

Definition: An enumeration is a variation on the same theme, such as, "Tell Mom he won't let me play" and "Tell Dad" (both are telling someone). Similarly, "Hit him" and "Kick him" are both ways to hurt someone.

Technique: When you hear an enumeration, classify the responses. In this case, say, "Telling Mom" and "Telling Dad" are kind of the SAME because they are both telling someone. Can you think of something DIFFERENT than 'telling someone'?"

Apparently Irrelevant Response

Definition: An apparently irrelevant response is a statement that does not appear to solve the problem, such as, "She could walk away."

Technique: Ask, "How will that help to solve the problem?" If your child says, "Then he'll feel sorry for her and let her play," that is actually a relevant solution. But if your child says, " 'Cause she can't have it," then you can say, "She *could* walk away. But the idea of this game is to think of a way to get to play with the video game."

Recording Responses

Write down what your child says in the "Thinking Clouds" provided on page 144. Even if she or he cannot read, doing so sends a message that his or her ideas are important. In order to help your child learn to distinguish responses that can and cannot solve the problem, do not record truly irrelevant responses.

Ending the Lesson

After all solutions are offered, say, "You've thought of lots of ways to solve this problem. You're a good problem solver. And you're going to get even better."

If only one or two solutions were given, say, "You thought of a (some) solution(s). You're going to be a very good problem solver."

Ways to Handle Common Behaviors

If you are doing these exercises with more than one child, watch for the Dominator, one who doesn't let the other(s) get a word in edgewise, as well as the Mimicker, who simply repeats what another child says.

Handling a Dominator
Say, "How does _____ feel if you take ALL the turns and _____ does not get any turns?"

Handling a Nonresponder
One way to help such a child is to give him or her a puppet and ask "Allie the Alligator" (or some such nickname) for an idea. Sometimes "Allie" will tell you a solution even if the child won't.

Handling a Mimicker

If this child is normally a verbal responder, say, "Oh, I know you can think of a DIFFERENT idea." If this child is shy or otherwise not very verbal, say, "Good, you told us too." For the child who is just beginning to respond verbally, instead of pushing, reinforce the fact that she or he said something. In time, this child will come up with different ideas and will feel proud instead of pressured.

Sample Demonstration Sheet: The Video Game

❧

The examples below will show you how to ask your child for solutions, how to probe for enumerations, how to record responses (including not recording apparently irrelevant ones), and one way to end the lesson.

Purpose

To help children think of alternative solutions to a problem.

Directions

Use figure 22 (as shown on page 145). Do not write in the sample Thinking Clouds on page 143. They are presented here only to show you how these lessons work.

Parent Script

Today's ICPS game is to try to solve a problem.

Let's pretend this girl *(point)* wants this boy *(point)* to let her play the video game. What does this girl want this boy to do? *(Child repeats problem.)*

OK. Listen carefully.

What can the girl do so the boy will let her play with the video game? *(Sample response: "Ask him." Record that answer in a "Thinking Cloud", as shown.)*

That's *one* way. Now the idea of the game is to think of lots of DIFFERENT ways the girl can solve this problem. I'm going to write down ALL of your ideas. Let's try to fill up ALL the "Thinking Clouds."

(Sample response: "Give him candy." Record in a new Thinking Cloud, and say): Now you have two ways. Can you think of way number three?

(If child says, "Give him gum" [enumeration], record it in the same Cloud as "Give him candy," then say): Giving him candy and giving him gum are kind of the SAME BECAUSE they are both giving something. Can you think of something DIFFERENT than giving something?

(Sample response: "I won't play with you anymore." Record it in a new Thinking Cloud, then say): Now you have three ways. She can ask him, way number one, OR give him candy or gum, way number two, OR she can tell him she won't play with him anymore, that's way number three. I bet you can think of way number four. *(If needed):* What else can the girl DO? What else can she SAY?

(If child says, "She could cry," ask): How would that help her get to play with the video game?

(If the child answers, " 'Cause she can't have it," do not record it. Crying for this reason is irrelevant because it is merely a reaction to not being able to play, not a way to get the boy to let her have a turn.)

If your child offers more solutions than there are Thinking Clouds, just write them on a separate sheet of paper.

Note: After your child's first relevant response, be sure to acknowledge it by saying, "That's *one* way. The idea of this game is to think of lots of ways to solve this problem." If you just ask for a different way without this statement, your child might think you didn't like what he or she said and might stop thinking of more ways.

Because it is a process that you are trying to develop—that is, *how* children think, not what children think—try to avoid saying, "That's a good idea." Say, "That's a different idea," or "Good thinking." Children will learn to think about whether or not their ideas are good ones in the next Parent's Pages, "I Can Problem Solve: Consequential Thinking." Also, by saying "Good idea," children might not see a need to think of more solutions that may be helpful the next time a similar problem arises.

What Else Can She Do?: The Video Game

❧

Purpose

To help children think of alternative solutions to a problem.

Directions

Use figure 22.

Parent Script

Today's ICPS game is to try to solve a problem.

Let's pretend this girl *(point)* wants this boy *(point)* to let her play with the video game. What does this girl want the boy to do? *(Child repeats problem.)*

OK. Listen carefully.

What can the girl do so the boy will let her play with the video game?

(Record your child's answers in the Thinking Clouds at the right. Follow script as shown on the sample Demonstration Sheet on pages 142–143.)

Note: Your children may enjoy coloring the pictures in activities not specifically designed for coloring. In fact, they may think of more ideas if you ask the question again while they are actively involved in the coloring.

Fig. 22

What Else Can He Do?
The Truck

Purpose

More on alternative-solution thinking.

Directions

Use figure 23.

Parent Script

What is happening in this picture?

Yes, this boy *(point)* is grabbing this truck from this boy *(point)*.

Let's say the boy who is grabbing wants to play with the truck, and he decides that to get it, he'll grab it. Grabbing is *one* way to get to play with the truck.

What else can he do to get to play with the truck?

(Follow the same script as the previous problem and write child's solutions in the Thinking Clouds to the left.)

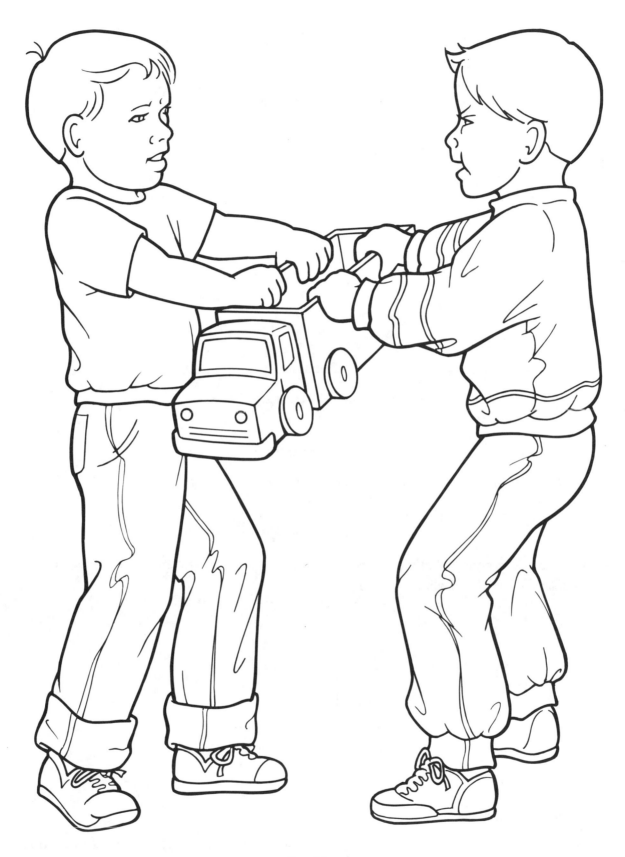

Fig. 23

ICPS Tic·Tac·Toe

❦

Purpose

To give children practice in generating solutions and identifying enumerations.

Directions

Two children can play this game, or you and your child can play.

Parent Script

Here are some pencils. Let's play a game of tic-tac-toe. *(Play a game or two to make sure your child [children] know how to play.)*

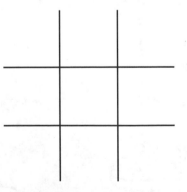

Now we're going to play this game a new way.

(If you're playing with one child): (Michael), do you want to be the X or the O? OK, you'll be the *(child's choice)* and I'll be the (the remaining choice).

I'm going to tell you a problem. (Michael), you'll think of a solution to the problem. If that solution will help to solve it, you choose a square and put in your (X).

Then I get a turn. I have to think of a DIFFERENT solution, and if I do, I put an (O) in a square I choose.

When it's your turn again, you have to think of a DIFFERENT solution from any given by you or by me, so listen carefully. If I give a solution that is kind of the SAME, try to catch me. And I'll try to catch you too.

(Give one or two enumeration solutions [solutions that are kind of the same] on purpose. If needed, prompt your child to "catch" you. Then ask or, if needed, explain how they are kind of the same.)

If two children are playing, repeat the directions, using the names of the children. Your role will be to supervise the game. Do not add solutions of your own.

SAMPLE GAME

Parent Script

First I'll show you how to play.

The problem is: John was playing with JoAnn's new kite and he tore it. Her beautiful new kite was all in pieces.

John is afraid JoAnn will be angry.

The question is: What can John do or say so JoAnn will NOT be ANGRY?

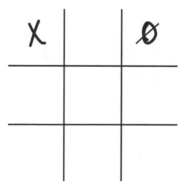

First, the child playing X says, "John could glue it," and he chooses a square. *(Child writes the X in a square, as shown.)* Then O says, "John could tape it" and chooses a square. *(Child writes the O in the square as shown.)*

(Did X catch this enumeration? If he caught it, ask): Why are these kind of the SAME? Now X gets an extra turn because he caught O's solution that was kind of the SAME.

(If X did not catch it, say): Oh, these are kind of the SAME. Can either of you tell me why? (If needed, say): Tape it and glue it are both ways to fix it.

O loses the square because he gave a solution that was kind of the SAME as the one X gave, and I'm going to cross (erase) the O out (*as shown*). But now it is O's turn again because X didn't catch that solution. O gets another chance.

(*Continue the game now, until someone gets a row of Xs or Os.*)

Hint: Any seemingly irrelevant response should be probed: "How can that help to solve this problem?" If still irrelevant, do not include it and ask the same child for another solution.

OK. Now we're going to play the game again.

The problem is: Robert wants to play hide and seek, but his sister doesn't want to play.

X, what is your idea? What can Robert do or say to solve his problem?

(*Any square with an enumeration that is crossed out or erased is still open for a new solution by either player.*)

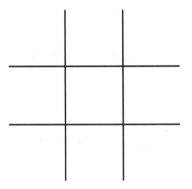

Think of a new problem and repeat the game as many times as the children desire. You can make up more tic-tac-toe sheets, if needed.

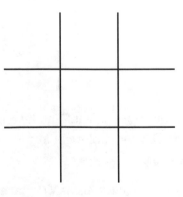

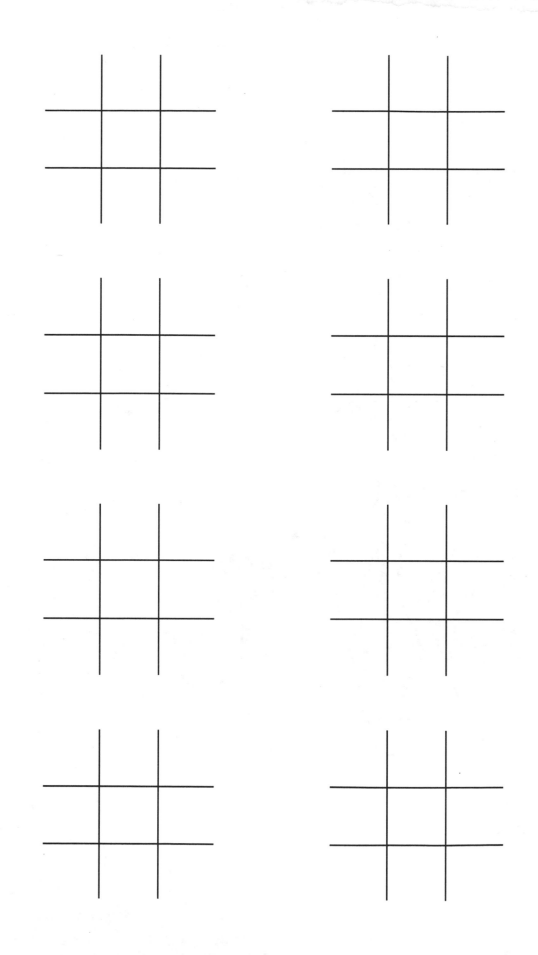

Fig. 24

What Else Can They Do?: The TV Show

❧

Purpose

Alternative solution thinking.

Directions

Use figure 24.

Parent Script

What is happening in this picture?

Yes, these kids are arguing over which TV show to watch.

On *this* set, can they watch DIFFERENT shows at the SAME TIME?

What can they do to solve the problem? What's one way?

Continue the same script you followed for "The Video Game" and "The Truck."

SAMPLE PARENT AND CHILD EXCHANGE

Below is another typical problem between two children. Sometimes the way a parent talks to a child sounds demanding and belittling, even when explanations for behavior are given.

"I had it first."

Child 1: I had it first!

Child 2: No, I had it first.

Dad: Now, look, I can't help you if you don't tell me who really had it first.
 (Dad will never know.)

Child 1: Me, me!

Dad: If you two grab like that, you won't have any friends and you'll break toys and Daddy will be mad and you'll both end up in your rooms.
(The children probably didn't hear a word of this.)

Later:

Dad: You're grabbing again. Don't you ever learn? You know Daddy is mad.
What do I have to do to teach you to share and be nice to each other?
If you don't learn to be nice to each other, how are you going to learn to be nice to other people? *(They probably didn't hear this either.)*

In the space provided, write a RUNG 4 ICPS dialogue to help these children solve this problem. Also write how they might respond. Try to include questions about each other's feelings and questions that use the word *DIFFERENT*.

RUNG 4 ICPS DIALOGUE

Directions

Fill in who is doing the talking (e.g., Mom, Dad, or children). See sample dialogue on the next page.

PERSON

_____   _____

            _____

_____   _____

            _____

_____   _____
_____   _____
_____   _____
_____   _____
_____   _____
_____   _____
_____   _____
                     _____

SAMPLE RUNG 4 ICPS DIALOGUE

Dad: Robert, how do you feel when Debbie grabs things from you?

Robert: Mad.

Dad: Debbie, how do *you* feel now?

Debbie: Mad.

Dad: Grabbing is *one* way to get your toy back. What happens when you grab toys?

Debbie: We fight.

Dad: Can either of you think of a *different* way so you won't fight?

Robert: I can show her how to play with it.

Debbie: We can play together.

This is a dialogue with a four- and a six-year-old thinking about feelings and how to solve the problem. Dad helped them do that with a few simple questions.

Question: Had this father said, "If you two can't share your toy,
I'll put it away so neither of you can have it," which rung would he be on?

Answer: RUNG 1. This statement threatens children into submission.

Question: What does a RUNG 4 ICPS Dialogue, such as the one this father used,
do that threatening to take the toy away does not do?

Answer: ICPS Dialoguing helps children think about their own and other's feelings,
what happens next (the consequences), and a different way to solve the problem.
In the next section, we will focus on consequential thinking, an integral part of the
full problem-solving process.

Note: After everyone in the family is comfortable with problem solving, you can simply say to your children, "Can you ICPS this?"

Figs. 25a, 25b, and 25c

Before/After:
What Happens Next?

❧

Purpose

To understand sequencing in problems with other children, and to set the stage for consequential thinking.

Materials

Crayons, any three colors

Directions

Use figures 25a–c. The pictures are in incorrect order. Ask your child to color the squares under each picture as you ask each question.

Parent Script

Look at these pictures. Which one comes first? Color the square under it (red).

Then what? Color what happened next (green).

And then? Color how this story ends (blue).

What MIGHT have happened BEFORE the boy knocked down the blocks? Anything else?

 Was knocking down the blocks a GOOD IDEA or NOT A GOOD IDEA? WHY?

How does the girl feel?

Did the girl feel that way BEFORE or AFTER the boy knocked down the blocks?

What MIGHT have happened AFTER the boy knocked down the blocks?

I CAN PROBLEM SOLVE: CONSEQUENTIAL THINKING

As in the previous section on asking for solutions, it is important to remember a few key points. The first exercise that you'll use to help develop this thinking skill is about a boy who is pushing a girl off a bike because she won't let him ride it (shown in figure 26 on page 162).

Some Definitions of Terms and Techniques

Consequence

Definition: A consequence is a reaction in direct response to an act performed by another person. For example, if the boy pushes the girl off the bike, she MIGHT "Cry," "Tell her mother," or "Not be his friend anymore."

Technique: After one consequence is given, say, "That's *one* thing that MIGHT happen next. The idea of *this* game is to think of lots of DIFFERENT things that MIGHT HAPPEN NEXT IF (he pushes her off the bike). "What else MIGHT happen next?"

Enumeration

Definition: As with solutions, enumerations are consequences that are kind of the same. For example, if the boy is pushing the girl, responses such as "She'll hit him," "Knock him down," or "Kick him" are kind of the SAME because they could lead to potential harm.

Technique: When you hear an enumeration, say, "Hitting him, knocking him down, or kicking him are all kind of the SAME BECAUSE they could ALL hurt him. Can you think of something DIFFERENT that MIGHT happen?"

Acceptable and Questionable Responses

Definition: Acceptable and questionable responses include those that (a) may not be connected to the question posed, but (b) are really solutions. For example, if your child says "He could ask her," the response is another way the *boy* could get to ride the bike, not a consequence of pushing.

Technique: If the response is clearly irrelevant, ask, "WHY do you think that MIGHT happen?" If the response is really a new solution, say, "He *could* ask her. But now I want to know what else MIGHT happen IF he pushes her off the bike. What else MIGHT the *girl* do OR say?"

Unclear Responses
Definition: Unclear responses are those that may or may not be relevant, depending upon what your child has in mind or which character is doing the act.

Technique: If, for example, your child simply says, "Hit," it could be a solution or a consequence depending on who says it. If it's the boy who says it, it's a *solution*, a way to get the girl off the bike so he can have it. If it's the girl who says it, then it's a *consequence* because she's going to hit in retaliation to being pushed off the bike. Similarly, a response such as "Tell the teacher" is a *solution* if the boy is seeking help to get the bike and a *consequence* if the girl wants to get the boy in trouble. Your child may not be able to verbalize all of this. If you are unsure, just ask him or her to point to which child in the picture would say that. If your child points to the girl, assume it's a *consequence*. If to the boy, say, "Hitting (or telling the teacher) is a way for the boy to get to the bike. In this game, I want to know what MIGHT happen next if the boy pushes the girl off the bike. You know, what MIGHT the girl do or say?"

Recording Consequences

List a solution and then dramatically draw arrows to display the connection between a solution and a consequence as shown in the Sample Demonstration Sheet that follows.

Ending the Lesson

After all consequences are offered, ask, "Is pushing her off to get to ride the bike a GOOD IDEA or NOT A GOOD IDEA?" *(Child answers.)* "WHY?"

Ask for a new solution for the boy to get to ride the bike, then ask for consequences to that new solution (what the girl MIGHT do or say).

Sample Demonstration Sheet: He's Pushing Me!

❧

Purpose

To help children think of consequences, the impact of behavior on one's self and on others.

Directions

Use figure 26, shown on page 162. Do not write on these sample sheets. They are presented here for demonstration only.

Parent Script

What's happening in this picture?

Yes, this boy is pushing this girl off the bike BECAUSE she won't let him ride it.

Today's ICPS game is about what might happen when someone does something.

What MIGHT happen next, AFTER the boy pushes the girl off?

I'm going to write down what you say MIGHT happen next.

(If child says, "She might push him back," say): OK, that's *one* thing that MIGHT happen. I'm going to draw an arrow for ALL the things you can think of that MIGHT happen.

In the space below dramatically *draw an arrow from the solution to the consequence as you repeat and write the consequence your child tells you.*

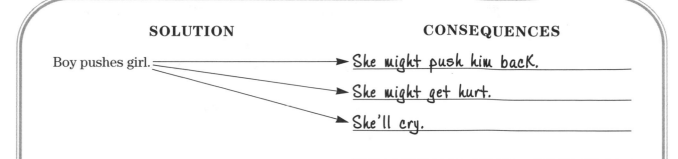

SOLUTION	CONSEQUENCES

Boy pushes girl. → She might push him back.

→ She might get hurt.

→ She'll cry.

The idea is to think of lots of things that MIGHT happen next if the boy pushes the girl off the bike. What else MIGHT happen?

(Sample response: "She might get hurt.")

(Record above as shown.) "Can you think of a third thing that MIGHT happen? Something she MIGHT do OR say?"

(Sample response: "She'll cry.")

(Record above as shown.)

(After all consequences are offered, say): Lots of things can happen from one solution. Is pushing her off the bike a GOOD IDEA or NOT A GOOD IDEA?

WHY (IS that/is that NOT) a GOOD IDEA?

(If desired, ask for another solution and repeat the process.)

What can he do that is DIFFERENT from pushing her?

What Might Happen Next?:
He's Pushing Me!

❧

Purpose

To think of consequences, the impact of behavior on one's self and others.

Directions

Use figure 26.

Parent Script

What's happening in this picture?

Yes, this boy *(point)* is pushing this girl *(point)* off the bike BECAUSE she won't let him ride it.

Today's ICPS game is about what might happen when someone does something.

What MIGHT happen next, AFTER he pushes her off?

I'm going to write down what you say MIGHT happen next.

Fig. 26

Record your child's answers in the spaces provided on the next page. Follow questions and recording as shown on the Sample Demonstration Sheet. Draw arrows as you record your child's responses.

SOLUTION	CONSEQUENCES
Boy pushes girl.	_____
	_____
	_____
	_____
	_____

Hint: Did you catch *enumerations*? Did you tell your child that "She won't let him ride her bike" and "She won't let him play with her toys," for example, are kind of the SAME BECAUSE they're both about not letting him play with her things? Did you ask for something DIFFERENT that MIGHT happen?

Hint: Did you catch responses that were really *solutions*? Did you tell your child that "Ask her," for example, is a way that the boy could get the girl to let him ride the bike? Did you then say, "Now I want you to tell me what MIGHT happen next if the boy pushes her off the bike"?

Parent Script

Lots of things can happen from this one solution. Is pushing her off the bike a GOOD IDEA OR NOT A GOOD IDEA?

(Ask for another solution *and repeat the game.)*

SOLUTION	CONSEQUENCES
_____	_____
	_____
	_____
	_____
	_____

Is *(repeat child's second solution)* a GOOD IDEA OR NOT A GOOD IDEA?

(If child says that it is NOT a good idea, ask): Can you think of something that IS A GOOD IDEA?

_____

_____

Fig. 27

What Might Happen Next?: I Want the Boat!

❦

Purpose

To further strengthen consequential thinking.

Directions

Use figure 27.

Parent Script

What is happening in this picture?

WHY might this girl be hitting this boy?

Any other reason? Another BECAUSE?

What MIGHT happen next AFTER she hits him?

I'm going to write down ALL the things you say. (*Use same techniques as the last game.*)

SOLUTION	CONSEQUENCES
Girl hits boy.	

Is hitting him a GOOD IDEA OR NOT A GOOD IDEA?

(Ask for another solution and repeat the game.)

SOLUTION	**CONSEQUENCES**
_____	_____
	_____
	_____
	_____
	_____

Is *(repeat child's second solution)* a GOOD IDEA OR NOT A GOOD IDEA?

(If child says that it is NOT a good idea, ask): Can you think of something that IS A GOOD IDEA?

_____

_____

A Feeling Story:
The Teddy Bear

❧

Purpose

To focus on feelings and consequences.

Directions

Use figures 28a–c. Read the story below and point to the pictures as you read. Use a different voice for each story character. Ask your child to draw in the squares provided faces that represent how each character feels at that point in the story.

Fig. 28a

Parent Script

Here's Ruby and she says, "Thanks Mom (Dad) for my new teddy bear. It talks. It says 'Hello, Ruby. My name is Petie. I can dance. See how I dance.'"

Ruby says, "I feel very _____ (child responds)."

Willie comes and says, "Hi, Ruby. Can I play with your new teddy bear?" And Ruby says, "OK."

Willie is playing with the teddy bear and sings, "La la la la. I'm pulling the string to make him talk. Oh-oh. I pulled it too hard and it broke. Now Petie can't talk."

Fig. 28b

Fig. 28c

Now Willie feels _____ *(child draws face in square).*

Ruby yells, "You broke my teddy bear!
Now he can't talk. I feel _____ ."

Ruby says, "I never want to play with you again, Willie!"
Willie feels _____ .

Willie says to himself, "I think I have to solve a problem." What can Willie think of? Ruby is very angry. What can Willie do or say so Ruby will NOT be so angry?

(Child answers.)

Is that a good idea? What MIGHT happen next IF Willie does (says) that? Think of lots of things that MIGHT happen.

_____

_____

_____

_____

_____

Ask your child for more solutions and then let him or her finish the story so everyone feels HAPPY.

_____

_____

_____

_____

_____

Fig. 29

What Might Happen Next?: The Painting

❧

Purpose

To continue practicing consequential thinking.

Directions

Use figure 29.

Parent Script

WHY MIGHT the girl be spilling the paint on the boy's picture?

What MIGHT happen AFTER she spills paint on the other boy's picture?

I'm going to write down all the things you say. *(Use arrows as before.)*

SOLUTION	CONSEQUENCES
Girl spills paint on boy's picture.	_____
	_____
	_____
	_____
	_____

Parent Script

Is spilling paint on the boy's picture a GOOD IDEA OR NOT A GOOD IDEA?

(Ask for another solution and repeat the game.)

SOLUTION	CONSEQUENCES
_____	_____
	_____
	_____
	_____
	_____

Is *(repeat child's second solution)* a GOOD IDEA OR NOT A GOOD IDEA?

(If child says that it is NOT a good idea, ask): Can you think of something that IS A GOOD IDEA?

_____

_____

SOLUTION/CONSEQUENCE PAIRING

The previous problem-solving games were designed to help children get used to the idea of thinking of many solutions and consequences in real-life problem situations. With flexibility in thinking, and more than one solution to try, children are now ready to link a consequence with each solution that comes to mind. Your child will become able to choose from a variety of solutions on the basis of whether one is or is not a good idea, and what might happen next.

Techniques

1. State the problem, or have your child state it.
2. Ask for one solution to the problem.
3. Ask for one consequence to *that* solution.
4. If the consequence is relevant, ask for a new solution and draw a connecting arrow.
5. Ask for the consequence of the new solution, etc.

Recording Solution/Consequence Pairs

Write down what your child says (as shown below) in the spaces provided on page 176.

Solution 1 <u>Ask her.</u>   ⟶ Consequence 1 <u>She'll say no.</u>
Solution 2 <u>Will invite to party.</u> ⟶ Consequence 2 <u>She won't come.</u>
Solution 3 _____ ⟶ Consequence 3 _____

Example: One Girl Won't Play with Another Anymore.

Parent: What could this girl do or say?
Child: Ask her.
Parent: And what MIGHT happen if she does that?
Child: She'll say no.

Continue to record each solution and its consequence before going on to the next solution.

Parent: And what else could she do? Way number two. (*If needed*): What could she *say*?
Child: I'll invite you to my birthday party.
Parent: And what MIGHT happen then?
Child: She won't come.

Enumerations and Unclear or Apparently Irrelevant Responses

Treat variations on a common theme and responses that are unclear or apparently irrelevant the same way you would alternative solutions and consequences.

Fig. 30

What Might Happen
If I Do That?:
Robin Won't Play with Me

❧

Purpose

To encourage children to think of a specific solution and how it might have an immediate impact on themselves and others.

Directions

Use figure 30.

Parent Script

Let's pretend that this girl *(point)* won't play with this girl anymore.

Can you think of a reason, a BECAUSE?

_____

_____

Any other reason, another BECAUSE?

_____

_____

OK. The problem is that this girl *(point)* won't play with this girl *(point)* BECAUSE *(repeat child's reason, such as, "She has a new friend," "They had a fight," etc.)*.

OK. Now, listen carefully. This is a new question. Tell me one thing this girl can do or say to solve this problem, AND one thing that MIGHT happen next if she does that.

I'm going to write down your solutions on this side of the paper *(point to left side)*.

I'm going to put what MIGHT happen next over here *(point to right side. Draw arrows in the usual way.)*

SOLUTION	**CONSEQUENCES**
_____	_____
_____	_____
_____	_____
_____	_____
_____	_____

What Might Happen If I Do That?: My Own Story

❧

Purpose

To give more practice in thinking about feelings and consequences.

Materials

Pencil or crayon

Directions

Write the story as your child tells it.

Parent Script

Today we're going to make up a story, a very special kind of story. I'm going to tell you two kinds of problems that kids have with each other. You decide which one you want to make up a story about. OR, you can choose a different problem if you'd like.

OK, here are the two problems.

1. A girl is always getting in trouble at school for talking to another girl during storytime.
2. A boy teases other kids and no one likes him anymore.

First, draw either (1) two kids talking to each other and a teacher trying to read a story to them, or (2) one kid teasing another, or (3) a problem you choose.

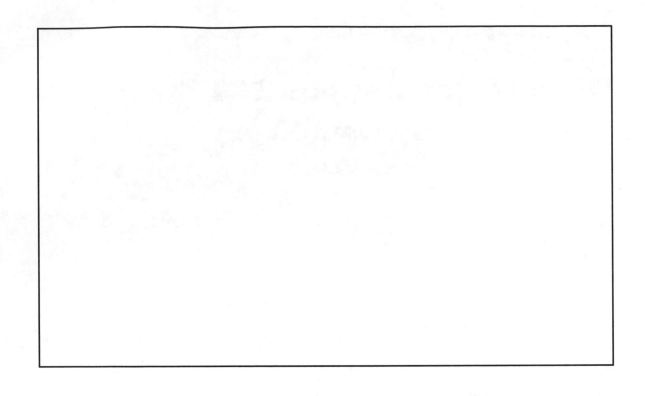

Now tell me your story and I'll write it down. You have to use two words that tell how someone in the story feels. You can use the words *HAPPY, SAD, ANGRY, AFRAID, FRUS-TRATED,* or *PROUD.* You can use more than two of these words, but try to use at least two DIFFERENT feeling words in your story.

(Write your child's story below as your child tells it.)

_____

_____

_____

_____

_____

_____

_____

_____

_____

_____

Now let's try to solve this problem.

What can *(name character in story)* do to solve this problem? And what MIGHT happen if she (he) does that?

Hint: Remember, ask for a consequence to the first solution (and draw its corresponding arrow) before asking for a second solution, its consequence, and so forth.

SOLUTION   ### CONSEQUENCES

_____   _____

_____   _____

_____   _____

_____   _____

_____   _____

This is the last game in the workbook, but we can play any that you particularly liked again.

You've become a really good problem solver! How do you feel about that?

DATE _____

> **A Problem Solver**
> Able to negotiate
> to reach a goal,
> or able to wait for
> what she or he wants

———

Becoming a Problem Solver	*Becoming a Problem Solver*
Tries *more* than one solution. But, if fails, still retreats, gives up.	Tries *more* than one solution. But, if fails, still resorts to emotion.

———

Early Attempt to Problem Solve
Tries one solution.
If fails, walks away.

Early Attempt to Problem Solve
Tries one solution.
If fails, gets upset.

———

Nonthinking, Emotional Responses
crying
sullen
hovering
hiding

Nonthinking, Emotional Responses
arguing
fighting
hitting
curse words

———

Shy/Withdrawn

Aggressive

FINAL DIALOGUE REVIEW

Problem

Boy calls girl a name.

   Match each response on the left to the categories on the right.

WHAT PARENTS MIGHT SAY

1. How many times do I have to tell you not to call her names?
2. She feels angry when you do that.
3. Calling her a name is not nice. You tell her how you feel.
4. She won't be your friend if you should call her names like that.

5. Tell her you're sorry.

6. What happened BEFORE you called her a name?
7. How do you think she feels when you call her a name?
8. And what happened AFTER you called her a name?
9. Can you think of a DIFFERENT way to tell her how you feel?

CATEGORIES

Genuine Information-Seeking Question: _____

Non-Information-Seeking Question: _____

Feelings:
   Asking _____
   Telling _____

Solutions:
   Asking _____
   Telling _____

Consequences:
   Asking _____
   Telling _____

Check your answers with those on the next page.

ANSWERS TO FINAL DIALOGUE REVIEW

Problem

Boy calls girl a name.

Match each response on the left to the categories on the right.

WHAT PARENTS MIGHT SAY   **CATEGORIES**

1. How many times do I have to tell you not to call her names?

   Genuine Information-Seeking Question: __6__

2. She feels angry when you do that.

3. Calling her a name is not nice. You tell her how you feel.

   Non-Information-Seeking Question: __1__

4. She won't be your friend if you should call her names like that.

   Feelings:

   Asking __7__

5. Tell her you're sorry.

   Telling __2__

6. What happened BEFORE you called her a name?

   Solutions:

   Asking __9__

7. How do you think she feels when you call her a name?

   Telling __3, 5__

8. And what happened AFTER you called her a name?

   Consequences:

   Asking __8__

9. Can you think of a DIFFERENT way to tell her how you feel?

   Telling __4__

FINAL DIALOGUE REVIEW

Problem

Now try the same exercise with a problem your child faces. On the left, write down what you do or say and match that statement to its category on the right.

YOUR RESPONSES

1. _____
   _____

2. _____
   _____

3. _____
   _____

4. _____
   _____

5. _____
   _____

6. _____
   _____

7. _____
   _____

8. _____
   _____

9. _____
   _____

CATEGORIES

Genuine Information-Seeking Question: _____
Non-Information-Seeking Question: _____

Feelings:
   Asking _____
   Telling _____

Solutions:
   Asking _____
   Telling _____

Consequences:
   Asking _____
   Telling _____

REAL-LIFE ANECDOTES: CHILD/CHILD PROBLEMS

Since completing Part 2 of this workbook, do your children behave or speak differently to their brothers and sisters or to neighborhood children? For example, if someone has something they want, what do your children say? Do they use ICPS words? Do your children, for example, tease or bully others less because they now think about how others feel?

Write down any changes you've noticed in your children:

_____

_____

_____

_____

_____

_____

_____

_____

_____

Use the space below to keep track of any other anecdotes or behaviors relating to child/child situations—both positive, non-problem-solving situations or conflict and other problem situations.

_____

_____

_____

_____

_____

_____

_____

_____

_____

_____

WHEN ACTIVITIES AND GAMES ARE COMPLETED

Congratulations! You have now completed the activities and games in *Raising a Thinking Child Workbook*. This makes you an official ICPS family. You'll find a special certificate at the end of this book. Frame it and hang it on your wall. You and your family can feel proud that you have taken the time and effort so that your *children* will:

- be more sensitive to their own and others' feelings,
- think of more than one way to solve a problem,
- anticipate the consequences of their acts upon themselves and others,
- be aware of good times and not good times to act, and
- better cope with frustration when they cannot obtain their wishes;

and *you* will:

- find out your children's view of the problem,
- help your children think about their own and others' feelings in a problem situation,
- help your children to think of alternative solutions to problem situations,
- help your children think about the consequences of their actions,
- encourage your children to evaluate their solutions by whether an idea is or is not a good one.

Don't stop ICPSing.

Continue to dialogue with your children the problem-solving way so they can continue to associate how they think with what they do. Any of the activities and games in this workbook can be repeated as often as your children desire, or they can make up their own, and you can create some as well. If you want additional information about the program, or more examples and exercises, you can find them in the original book, *Raising a Thinking Child* (Henry Holt and Company, 1994; paperback, Pocket Books, 1995).

I'd love to hear about your experiences with ICPS. Please feel free to share your stories and anecdotes with me by sending them to Myrna B. Shure, Ph.D., Medical College of Pennsylvania and Hahnemann University, Broad and Vine MS 626, Philadelphia, PA 19102.

USING THE
ICPS WORD-PAIR POSTERS

❧

At the back of this workbook are posters with illustrations for some of the ICPS word pairs that you have used. These posters can be used in several ways:

- Select a word pair of the day and place its poster on your refrigerator or some other convenient place. Repeat this for subsequent word pairs.

- Let your children be the teacher, making up sentences using these posters.

- Use these words in positive, everyday situations, not just in problem situations, so that they will be associated with fun and your children will be excited about using them to settle disputes and solve other kinds of problems that come up with you, other adults, and other children.

- Duplicate the blank poster sheet and create your own word-pair posters.

- Let your child draw faces on the posters with blank faces.

ICPS DIALOGUE REMINDERS

You may wish to place the following two pages in a visible place as reminders of the dialoguing process. Remember, there are no hard-and-fast rules for asking these questions. Once you and your children are familiar with ICPS dialogues, you can tailor them to your own unique problems.

PARENT/CHILD PROBLEMS

Can I talk to you AND to _____ AT THE SAME TIME?

Is that A GOOD PLACE to _____? *(examples: leave your toys, fingerpaint, etc.)*

Can you think of a DIFFERENT place to _____?

Is this A GOOD TIME to _____? *(example: ask me to read you a story)*

When IS A GOOD TIME to _____?

Can you think of something DIFFERENT to do while you wait?

Can you think of a DIFFERENT way to tell me how you feel? *(examples: child is whining, throwing a temper tantrum, using undesirable words)*

How do you think I feel when you _____? *(examples: don't listen, interrupt me, don't clean your room)*

Is that a GOOD IDEA? *(examples: throwing ball in house, writing on wall)*

What MIGHT happen if you do that?

How will I feel if that happens?

How will you feel if that happens?

What can you do so that will NOT happen?

CHILD/CHILD PROBLEMS

What happened? What's the matter? *(asks for child's view of the problem)*

What happened BEFORE (you hit him)? *(a nonthreatening way of asking "why")*

How do you think he felt when you (e.g., hit him, took his toy)? *(helps child to think of other's feelings)*

What happened when you (hit him, took his toy, yelled at your sister to stop bugging you)? *(helps child think of consequences)*

How did you feel when that happened? *(child's feelings are important too)*

Can you think of a DIFFERENT way to (get to play with the toy, tell your brother how you feel, tell your sister to stop bugging you)? *(child thinks of alternative solutions)*

Is that a GOOD IDEA? What MIGHT happen if you do that? *(child evaluates new solution)*

Do you have another idea too? *(child can try another way, if needed)*

Note: After a while, just asking, "Can you think of a DIFFERENT way to . . ." is all you need. Your children now understand that they need to ICPS.

A LITTLE QUIZ

❧

Now that you are an ICPS family, see how far you've come as an ICPS parent to raise a thinking child. Below are some of the key concepts of this approach for review. Circle what you think is (are) the correct answer(s) for each question. (The answers appear on page 191.)

1. Conflicts are
   a) problems to be solved
   b) annoyances to be dealt with quickly and gotten rid of
   c) purposeful behaviors to annoy you
   d) all of the above

2. Two goals of the games and activities you have performed with your child(ren) are to
   a) teach the language of problem solving
   b) teach language development to young children
   c) teach the process of thinking for solving everyday problems
   d) teach alternative solutions to everyday problems

3. The word *not* is included as part of ICPS learning because
   a) children will understand when we tell them not to do something
   b) it will add to their language development
   c) children will be able to decide whether an idea is or is not a good one
   d) we can tell them more solutions to problems

4. The words *same* and *different* are part of ICPS because
   a) children can distinguish which solutions are truly different and which ones are similar to each other
   b) they help children think about the idea that there is more than one way to solve a problem
   c) both of the above
   d) neither of the above

5. Two reasons we teach concepts of emotions are
   a) we want children to recognize and be sensitive to their own feelings
   b) we want children to recognize and be sensitive to the feelings of others
   c) we want to make children feel better
   d) we don't want children to become too selfish

6. When a child says "he can ask" for a toy, an ICPS parent might say:
   a) That's a good idea.
   b) Good thinking.
   c) both of the above
   d) neither of the above

7. When a child interrupts on the phone, two things an ICPS parent might say are:
   a) I'm talking to my friend. Why don't you watch TV while you wait?
   b) I'm talking to my friend. Can I talk to you and to my friend at the same time?
   c) I feel angry when you interrupt me when I'm on the phone.
   d) Can you think of something different to do while you wait?

8. When a child grabs a toy from another, three things an ICPS parent might say are:
   a) Do *not* grab toys. You must learn to share.
   b) I feel angry when you grab toys.
   c) How do you think I feel when you grab toys?
   d) You'll lose your friends if you grab toys.
   e) What might happen if you grab toys?
   f) Can you think of something different to do?

9. When a child comes home and says that another child hit her at school, an ICPS parent might say:
   a) Hit her back.
   b) Hit her back because I don't want you to be so timid.
   c) Don't hit her back, tell the teacher instead.
   d) If you don't hit her back, she'll keep on hitting her.
   e) Tell me what happened. What's the problem?

10. If your child is teasing or calling his brother names, two things an ICPS parent might say are:
   a) Go to time-out now!
   b) Your brother is angry when you talk to him like that.
   c) How do you think your brother feels when you talk to him like that?
   d) Can you think of a different way to talk to your brother?

11. It is important for children to be able to think for themselves because
   a) they are more likely to carry out their own ideas than those suggested or even explained by an adult
   b) they are less likely to give up too soon
   c) they will gain a sense of control over their lives
   d) people won't always be around to help them
   e) they will grow up as thinking, feeling human beings who are less likely to hurt themselves or other people
   f) all of the above
   g) Can you think of any other reasons? _____

   _____

Answers

1. *a*
2. *a* and *c* (words are for association with process of problem solving, not general language development, and not to teach specific solutions)
3. *c*
4. *c*
5. *a* and *b* (empathy requires caring about one's own feelings before true concern for others)
6. *b* (it's process, not content)
7. *b* and *d* (*a* and *c* are telling, not asking)
8. *c*, *e*, and *f* (*a* is RUNG 2, *b* and *d* are RUNG 3)
9. *e* (*a* and *c* are RUNG 2, *b* and *d* are RUNG 3)
10. *c* and *d*, (*a* as used here is punishment, on RUNG 1, *b* is RUNG 3)
11. *f*

❧ ICPS Resources ❧

For Parents

Shure, Myrna B., and Theresa Foy DiGeronimo. *Raising a Thinking Child: Help Your Young Child to Resolve Everyday Conflicts and Get Along with Others.* New York: Henry Holt, 1994 (hardcover).

_____. *Raising a Thinking Child: Help Your Young Child to Resolve Everyday Conflicts and Get Along with Others.* New York: Pocket Books, 1996 (paperback).

_____. *Raising a Thinking Child: Help Your Young Child to Resolve Everyday Conflicts and Get Along with Others.* New York: Bantam, Doubleday, Dell Audio Publishing, 1996 (spoken-word audio).

For Schools

Shure, Myrna B. *I Can Problem Solve (ICPS): An Interpersonal Cognitive Problem-Solving Program* [preschool]. Champaign, Ill.: Research Press, 1992.

_____. *I Can Problem Solve (ICPS): An Interpersonal Cognitive Problem-Solving Program* [kindergarten/primary grades]. Champaign, Ill.: Research Press, 1992.

_____. *I Can Problem Solve (ICPS): An Interpersonal Cognitive Problem-Solving Program* [intermediate elementary grades]. Champaign, Ill.: Research Press, 1992.

Is   Is Not

Who IS happy?
Who IS NOT happy?

And   Or

Is this girl standing AND stretching

OR is she standing AND jumping ?

Same Different

Are these boys playing with the SAME truck or a DIFFERENT truck?

Before After

Was this boy sad BEFORE

or AFTER his truck broke?

Good Time?

Is this a GOOD TIME or

NOT A GOOD TIME to ask

this girl to go outside and play?

Good Place?

Is this a **GOOD PLACE** or

NOT A GOOD PLACE for his toys?

at the Same Time

Can mom talk to her child and to her friend AT THE SAME TIME?